empower

publishing

Also from Empower Publishing

by Linwood Best

Best "Quotes"

Best "Sayings"

Thoughts on Paper

Learn to Listen & Listen to Learn

publish.empower.now@gmail.com

Simply Faith

By

Dr. Linwood Best

Empower Publishing
Winston-Salem

Empower Publishing
302 Ricks Drive
Winston-Salem, NC 27103

© 2025, Linwood Best. All rights reserved. This book may not be reproduced in whole or in part without written permission from the author, except by a reviewer who may quote brief passages in a review; nor may any part of this book be reproduced, stored in *a* retrieval system, or transmitted in any form or by any means electronic, mechanical, photocopying, recording, or other, without written permission from the author.

First Empower Publishing Books edition published
May, 2025
Empower Publishing, Feather Pen, and all production designs are trademarks of Indigo Sea Press, used under license.

Scripture, unless otherwise indicated, are taken from "The
Holy Bible, New International Version (NIV)
The Holy Bible, New King James Version (KJV)
Holy Bible, New Living Translation (NLT)
Holy Bible, English Standard Version (ESV)
Holy Bible, The Message (TM))
Cover design by Linwood Best
Manufactured in the United States of America
ISBN 978-1-63066-619-4

ACKNOWLEDGEMENT

Giving honor to God and to Jesus Christ, who reassured me that there was room at the cross for a broken sinner like me, and to the Holy Spirit, who continues to provide comfort to my soul until Jesus unfastens the heavens. I would like to express thanks to God for the privilege and opportunity to proclaim His word.

Reflections of my late mother, Alma R. Best, who showed love to me in her distinctive way. I am thankful to her for life. Truly, words can't express my love for you, mother.

To Mrs. Pearly Zachery (my 4th-grade teacher), who encouraged me "to be whatever you want to be but be yourself."

To Mrs. Lou Elliot, who was not my teacher, however, when we crossed paths, she would remind me to press on and not give up. She would say, "It is in you."

To the late Deacon William Faison, who was an example of what a godly man should be, both in word and deed. "We know nothing we have not learned from another teacher." I am beholden to all those who have had a part in teaching me, both academically and spiritually.

To my wife, Brenda, for her endless love, encouragement, patience, and support during the writing of this book and for our yesterdays, today, and forever.

To my grandmother-in-law Marie Smith (Granny), who, with love and kindness, led me to God's throne of grace when I was in darkness.

And to Christian Fellowship Church, my haven on earth family, who were instrumental in spreading the Good News. Thank you. Thank you for welcoming us in love and allowing me to pastor you. It is not by chance that God led us this way.

CONTENTS

PART I	Seems Everybody Got It	1
PART II	Transportation on Wheels	5
PART III	A Hard Head but an Open Door	15
PART IV	Scattered Thoughts May Land Anywhere	17
PART V	Self-Test	26
PART VI	Mental Exercise—Think on These Things	34
PART VII	But What Does This Really Mean	42
PART VIII	Determination vs. Faith	43
	Toolbox For Spiritual Development	65

RENEWING YOUR MIND
Simply Faith
Part I
Seems Everybody Got It

It is surprising how many people today are aware of the power, promises, health, help, and wealth of knowledge at our disposal supported by the Word of God and members of the Body of Christ; yet still suffer from doubt, unbelief, worry, and double-mindedness. Why? Could it be because of a misinterpretation of what faith is.

We use faith so loosely that it appears magical. We tend to say that almost anything and everything is faith. "I bought a car, and many other things I want are included." It is amazing how faith is defined when it comes to personal experiences, individual understanding, and spiritual or religious interpretation. You would be amazed at the response of a child when asked, "What is faith?" Of course, the response will be a wide range: "It is when my parents give me something I have asked for because I have been good, and they gave it to me." Is it because we've done something good? That could also be the answer of many adults, too. For some unfounded reason, we associate receiving with our contribution of good works. Biblically, that is far from the truth.

On the other hand, the word faith is used so offhandedly that you'd be disappointed not to think that we do so all the time. The focus of this book hopefully will make us conscious of the need to renew our mind to God's way of thinking, which will become normal. The Bible clearly distinguishes that God's ways are not like ours; His are better. Do we really understand, or do we underestimate, what FAITH really means? How do we get it, and then what we do with it will determine the victory and failure of life.

Faith requires courage. Therefore, in theory, faith is not cowardice; it has guts and is brave. It is true that if you want to get something accomplished, dare to do it, but it is more than simply saying it— it must have a backbone. The Word of God is the believer's backbone, making it simple to take Him at his word.

From a scriptural perspective, every good and perfect gift comes from God (James 1:17). Please note with caution and care what's stated in the verse, "Not every good gift, but good and perfect." By definition, good means worthy, blameless, moral, upright, virtuous, and noble. A gift is from God. However, it does not say the good only, but perfect also. Perfect means faultless, flawless, picture-perfect, seamless, unspoiled, unflawed, unadulterated, impeccable, complete, absolute, whole, total, entire, intact, exact, accurate, finished, spot-on, ideal, great, wonderful, and nothing wrong with it. In other words, it is just what the doctor ordered.

What I am trying to get across is that we so often say that this and/or that is a gift from God. There is a different view, however. We are instructed to be content in whatever state we are in (Philippians 4:11), and when God's gift is manifested, it becomes good and perfect. Therefore, the delay is not the denial of what is to be. The challenge is not to be distracted. The manifestation process gradually changes from the unseen to the seen. Faith is the focus until the desired request is granted. We begin to utilize our faith when in actuality the touchable is not seen. God must be the center of our request and vision for the manifestation of the unseen. We will discover this as we continue this journey of the God kind of faith. It is anticipated but yet to be seen.

When we get a picture of the thing hoped for, it represents what is anticipated until it is received. We must continue the process to see it in the heart and mind. For instance, a picture could possibly cause us to become anxious. Let's revert back to a childhood moment. "Wait until your birthday." What happens? Anxiety is at full speed by the very fact that we want

Simply Faith

and can't wait to get it. This is not God's way of receiving.

Faith is taking the word of God to be true and applying it as so. Faith is the substance (core) of things hoped for and the evidence (proof) of things not seen. It is not just saying words; instead, it requires the application of words. If we promise a child something, he or she will remind us of the promise. Why? To them the promise becomes reality. Although it is not seen, they take our word. Faith instructs us to do the same. Faith is taking God at his word. If we have a situation that is about to overtake us, what are we to do? People say, "Have faith in God.". How can we? When our vision is cloudy, that view will often distract us, causing doubt. How often have we thought during difficult times, if I can just make it home? Or if I only had a chance to talk to my mother, dad, or best friend, things would be better? What about waiting for an injury or illness to heal? What were our options? That's right; we had to wait or hope for the best. That's all I am suggesting is for us to take God at his word and wait, allowing God to manifest his possibilities.

Think of the many challenges we have faced. While they were not impossible, we were confronted with unproductive imagination. The thoughts of a letdown will always present themselves but let us stay the course and see the fulfillment of our petition. Faith's application is simply our obedience to God's directive or his words in action.

The Book of James says, "Faith without works is dead" (James 2:26). When faith is activated, then and only then can it truly be unpretentious. Otherwise, in the marketplace it would be referred to as counterfeit.

We have seen fruit that appeared to have been real only to discover that it was not. At our home, there was a bowl of (artificial) fruit on the table, and to my surprise, I saw teeth marks in a pear. When eating lunch one day, I inquired as to who had been tricked by the fruit. My granddaughter said it was me, Papa. Had it been real fruit, she could have enjoyed it. What a lesson learned; we can't go by sight. Likewise, when it comes to faith, we should not be sight- oriented. We laugh, but what a crash course made appropriate to her in just a few words.

From childhood, most of us thought outside the box. As youngsters', we said without reservation what we were going to do and/or become. What caused the deviations? Why did we give up or quit? Transitional thinking caused us to become nearsighted, farsighted, shortsighted, and our vision became blurred and often blinded. When we thought like children, our imagination was a reality to us, and it was the norm. What happened, maybe as we grew older, we began to overthink?

Simply Faith

Part II
Transportation on Wheels

There was a time when we needed to get another vehicle. We finally found a reasonable purchase but discovered that it was sold (there was a window sticker stating that it was). My wife said, I guess we must continue our search. Well, I said if it is on the lot, it is not sold. By the way, this was on the weekend, and the dealership was closed. What was I to do?

On Monday morning I called, and sure enough the salesperson confirmed that a tag was in the window that it had been sold. I asked, Sold? He said, Yes, sir, somebody put a deposit with the intent to buy the car Friday. Without hesitation, I asked if I could put a backup deposit just in case the person did not buy the car. This was not some super luxury auto (no frills, just a sedan that is purchased by most consumers). To his amazement, he replied, "Okay, but you need to come as soon as possible because this 'affordable' car won't be here long." He further stated that others were interested in the car (even some salespersons).

I ask if I could make a deposit over the phone with a credit card. Of course, was his reply. I will not belabor this any further; I got the car. How did this happen? I did not accept what was seen as faith. Otherwise, I could have accepted what I saw (the sold sign), and that would have resulted in a different outcome.

Faith is beyond feeling. It is not moved by the climate. It ignores doubt. Faith never debates with unbelief. It refuses to apologize about the truth. It will not be controlled by the masses nor dictated to by royalty but will listen to belief and "nothing wavering." Presumption will never win over assurance. You see, assurance is the reward of obedience. Assurance and obedience must not be in competition. Otherwise, doubt and defeat will be the tag team champions.

Nothing wavering is a term referred to in the Bible in the book of James. It compares wavering to a double-minded person and the ship on the sea and is tossed. (James 1:6-8).

If we merely respond to feeling rather than faith, we are cheating ourselves. This rationalization is a bedrock for disappointment, resulting in doubt and unbelief. What happens next is that failure becomes our taskmaster rather than simply availing ourselves of faith that leads to peace. Peace of mind makes faith simple and reduces or eliminates anxiety and despair. Faith illuminates the darkness, overcomes obstacles, and makes hearing possible and the view clearer.

This book is written not because I have mastered faith, nor do I think that it is possible to do so. However, you are invited into the world beyond sight, for there we will discover the reality of faith. From a scriptural perspective, however, it is the real world of God. Why or how so? Because Hebrews 11:1 says faith is the substance of things we hope for and the evidence of things not seen.

Take note of this definition, as it will serve as a reference throughout the book.

Many life challenges have given me a better understanding of faith's importance and the need for it. It is a delight for me to share with you just a little of what I believe will help you too.

We can never have too much or too little faith. God expects us to apply that which is given to us by him. When we feel that we don't have faith, remember that God has dealt to every man (mankind) the measure (enough) that's needed. Let's keep that also in mind as we venture into the arena of Simply Faith and Renewing the Mind.

You have a personal invitation to renew your mind and gain a better understanding and appreciation for this basic need and what has been afforded us. You may or may not have known this, but in Romans 12:3 For I say, through the grace given unto me, to every man that is among you, not to think of himself more highly than he ought to think, but to think soberly, according as God has dealt to every man the measure of faith. When you said, "I can do that." You did not have a clue how, but you somehow thought you could, and many times you did. It is because of the potential that has been made available to every man, "the measure of faith."

My aim is to expose, discuss, relate, and guide you into areas that you may have taken for granted. Perhaps you or someone you know has come short of what God has made available through his promises. If so, then let's begin to take a deliberate approach to receiving what is ours.

A mental note to practice is that faith can be compared to an operation manual, procedure, protocol, preflight instruction, conduct, or behavior. Similarly, you cannot use "one" ball for all sports. In order to play the game, you must understand the rules, the scoring process, and what equipment is required. Don't get tricked by reasoning: fear is the enemy of faith; therefore, it can be disguised. The primary requirement of faith is to be attentive. Attention to God will provide deliverance from doubt and distractions. Renewing your mind does not frighten you; it gives you confidence to walk by faith. The difference between a winner and a loser is quitting – giving up – throwing in the towel. Keep on until you get there.

To accomplish this, we must lay aside preconceived ideas and unfounded hypotheses. We should shun or dismiss unwelcome intrusions. Keep in mind that faith does not have a timeline. Faith does require us to wait and waiting entails confident expectation and active hope in the Lord and never passive resignation. This is instructed in scripture.

Isaiah 40:31 (KJV) but they that wait upon the LORD shall renew their strength; they shall mount up with wings as eagles; they shall run and not be weary and they shall walk, and not faint.

When we wait, our faith is perfected, as the eagle depicts the strength that comes from the Lord. Faith and patience support one's hope until there is a manifestation.

Many of us have heard of the power, promises, health, help, and wealth of knowledge that are in the Word of God. With that information, we still struggle with doubt, unbelief, worry, and double-mindedness. This happens when there is the exposure of scripture without experience or information without application. The Book of James revealed it to us when he said, "Be ye doers of the word and not hearers ONLY" (James 1:22). To do this, we must be willing to accept God's word. Otherwise, in the same passage (vv.23-24) it says, "For if any be a hearer of the word, and not a doer, he is like unto a man beholding his natural face in a glass: "For he behold himself, and goth his way, and straightway forgets what manner of man he was." Faith involves both hearing and doing.

How do you think most people would define the meaning of faith? It would be like having a tool that is used in times of trouble - a sort of catch-all word for everything, especially when there is a need for a quick fix. Dictionary.Com defines faith as confidence or trust in a person or thing or a belief that is not based on proof. God has provided us the ability to sightsee from His viewpoint. In so doing, we discover with expectation that God will perform all he has promised to us in Christ. God's word is the reality of things that cannot be seen by the natural eye. Therefore, we should say, Lord, help me not to get in the way of your working. In doing so, we will learn that His ways are not like ours nor His thoughts.

Again, in Hebrews 11:1 (NIV), faith is confidence in what we hope for and assurance about what we do not see. Keep in mind that this will be the foundation on which we will continue to build. Why did the Apostle Paul use the word "now" in his sentence? Faith must be now or is not faith until NOW arrives. You and I might be satisfied to say it without the ***now,*** but would it be acceptable? A closer look at the importance of ***now*** makes a big difference. When you have a desire, when do you want a response? NOW!

It is vital that we have clarity concerning now faith. You see, NOW gives permission to hope until it is fulfilled. In

Simply Faith

Romans 10:17, we discover that faith comes by hearing and hearing the word of God. I have heard people say, Pray that I have faith, which we cannot do. Why? Because we can only pray that the person will hear and receive God's word when presented. The question should be, Why is it necessary? In Hebrews 11:6, it says that without faith, it is impossible to please God. Before going any further, let's think about the statement. How could we accomplish anything if it is not pleasing to God? Huh? It is true, "With God, nothing shall be impossible."

Likewise, if we are not pleasing God, nothing can and will be possible. Faith pleases God, and He has given it to us, resulting in us showing our appreciation by pleasing him. Reciprocity typifies the balance of exchange. Biblically, it means we reap what we sow. Matthew 6:33 proves this even further; it says that we should seek God first, and all these things shall be added. When we seek the guidance of God, there will always be benefits. It may not be monetary, but there will be a more solid foundation resulting from the experience. Faith is what pleases God, and He takes pleasure in accommodating us. Therefore, our aim should be to please God by our act of faith. God sees our faith when it is invisible to the world. Depositing it into our memory bank assuredly will please God.

Can you imagine being reluctant to go to purchase an item, having the money to get it, yet doubting the possibility of obtaining it? What's hindering the exchange? We longed for it, but yet there is hesitation. In the natural sense, this would be a monetary exchange; however, in the spiritual sense, faith would be this necessary channel. Comparatively, it is the same principle needed for us to transact godly business. Instead of using money, we must use faith to exchange it for what is sought after.

An illustration of this is in Mark 11:22-24: "Have faith in God"–do what is said. Jesus's statements may have been strange to the hearers then and even so today. Nevertheless, they are words of instructions. Please note, we are to avoid doubt. This hurdle we must avoid.

When doubt shows up, do not converse with it; don't feed it; starve it. Doubt is a thief. It will rob you. Doubt will ask questions without an answer. Our reply to doubt is never acceptable anyway. Doubt is an unauthorized agent that is a distraction. This agent has investigative rights but cannot enforce anything without our permission. Furthermore, you have no answer, and how can you when you are waiting for the manifestation from God?

Jesus is saying, Believe you have received, but doubt is asking, Does this make sense? Faith will drown doubt out. Doubt will try to take your emotions into custody. Faith requires (attentive) hearing. Not any kind of hearing but hearing the word of God. This is a challenge, but this seemingly simple act will determine the outcome. Notice faith comes by hearing, not heard but hearing. This is a routine assignment that leads to effective communication with God. In doing so, we have an entrance to His presence where our request is made known.

Jesus said in Matthew 6:33-34 "But seek ye first the kingdom of God (this is where the rule of truth begins) and his righteousness, and all these things shall be added unto you." Have you ever hastened to find a swift solution or a quick fix only to see no end in sight? Jesus said that when we take thought or rush to get an answer (not necessarily the right one), we bypass the process of growth and development. When this happens, we waste time, resulting in being tired, baffled, and without clarification. This is the doorway for doubt to return to and possibly abort the process.

It has been said that we reap what we sow. The farmer understands that what he planted is exactly what he will get. He cannot plant tomatoes and get potatoes. Remember, seeking God first results in all these things being added-often more than we could have imagined.

Genesis 2:7-9 "And God formed man of the dust of the ground and breathed into his nostrils the breath of life, and man became a living soul. And the Lord God planted a garden

Simply Faith

eastward in Eden, and there he put the man whom he had formed. And out of the ground made the Lord God to grow every tree that is pleasant to the sight and good for food; the tree of life also in the midst of the garden, and the tree of knowledge of good and evil." In the beginning, God gave us the ability to communicate and comprehend. The disconnect then and today fails because we do not apply the interrelating knowledge of God.

When we try to figure things out, we end up with doubt, unbelief, fear, and confusion. Proverbs 3:5,6 says we are to trust God with all our heart and not lean to our own understanding. When we don't wait, we have a blurred view of what is to come. "Hast truly does make waste," and we are left disappointed and in disarray. Waiting is part of the process.

This was the characteristic of the lost (prodigal) son described in Luke 15:11-24 NIV, Jesus continued: "There was a man who had two sons. The younger one said to his father, 'Father, give me my share of the estate.' So, he divided his property between them. "Not long after that, the younger son got together all he had, set off for a distant country, and there squandered his wealth in wild living. After he had spent everything, there was a severe famine in that whole country, and he began to be in need. So, he went and hired himself out to a citizen of that country, who sent him to his fields to feed pigs. He longed to fill his stomach with the pods that the pigs were eating, but no one gave him anything. "When he came to his senses, he said, 'How many of my father's hired servants have food to spare, and here I am starving to death! I will set out and go back to my father and say to him, Father, I have sinned against heaven and against you. I am no longer worthy to be called your son; make me like one of your hired servants.' So, he got up and went to his father. "But while he was still a long way off, his father saw him and was filled with compassion for him; he ran to his son, threw his arms around him, and kissed him. "The son said to him, 'Father, I have sinned against heaven and against you. I am no longer worthy

11

to be called your son.' "But the father said to his servants, 'Quick! Bring the best robe and put it on him. Put a ring on his finger and sandals on his feet. Bring the fattened calf and kill it. Let's have a feast and celebrate. For this son of mine was dead and is alive again; he was lost and is found.' So, they began to celebrate.

It is time for us to come home; it is time for us to wash our minds of the dirt and pollution that has taken hold. How did this happen? How do we reverse the process? A change of heart and attitude based on God's word will enable these simple truths to become alive. What we learn and remember is that the son was in search of what was already his, but he had to wait. He's waiting now. We must be persuaded that there is a pathway to our answer and his provision. Waiting is an act of trust that is mandated, and God is not forgetful of his search and recovery plan for us.

We are told in scripture that God is good; He shall supply all our needs; He's our shepherd, and we shall not want. Still anxious, say, I can't wait. Keep in mind that faith is what we cannot see, but it is on the way. God is for us, and as we draw near to him, he will draw near to us (James 4:8-10). His timeline is not to be dictated by us; rather, we trust him to wait. Often, we presume that everybody is on the same page. We rush to make a point that is not understood and without a foundation. For example, how many times have you heard, "Just trust God"? It sounded good, but we were not there yet. It would be like having a Global Positioning System (GPS) that provides users with positioning, navigation, and timing (PNT) services and not knowing how to operate it. With such technology and many roads traveled, surprisingly we miss our turn. Thank God that when we miss our turn, it does not make our arrival late.

You may be reading this book, and you too are not there. For that reason, let's pause and address a very important issue. If you are not a Christian, if you do not have a clear understanding of your direction, if you feel unloved, without hope, fearful, or angry, if you feel like taking your life or have

Simply Faith

thought about it. If you are wondering when and where the ends will meet. Feelings and imagination can be detrimental. There is hope with a promise for you. "For God so loved the world (you) that he gave his only begotten son that whosoever believeth in him should not perish but shall have everlasting life." God sent Jesus (his son) into the world not to condemn the world (you) but that the world (you) through him might be saved (John 3:16).

If the truth be known, all of us need to be recused. Like a drowning individual, certified lifeguard or not, "Get me out, help!." Irrespective of your past, "God sent not his son Jesus into the world to condemn." In John 3:18 Jesus said, "He that believeth in him is not condemned but he that believeth not is condemned already, because he hath not believed in the name of the only begotten son of God." By the way, in Christ Jesus there is no condemnation. God's 911 will come to the rescue. This is factual, not emotional, and there is an invisible, outstretched hand to receive you just as you are. For real—for real. What better time and place to start the process of renewing your mind? There's no need to wait until the end of the book to acknowledge the need and have a better understanding of such a change. The Bible says that faith comes by hearing the word of God. It further says, in the Weymouth New Testament, "Everyone, without exception, who calls on the name of the Lord shall be saved." A special invitation will be extended throughout the book. For you, it is now.

Pray this prayer, and please don't try to figure it out. It is your act of faith before God. Between the two of you. You are that important. He's been waiting for this moment.

Pray, God, I could not satisfy myself. I have tried so hard to only return empty-handed. I need help. I was a sinner before I met you. Therefore, I confess with my mouth the Lord Jesus and believe with my heart that God has raised him (Jesus) from the dead for my salvation. I welcome this invitation for my salvation. Based on your promise, God, I take you at your word; therefore, I am saved. Thank you, Lord, for saving me.

This is found in Romans 10:9 and 10. What is happening is that God is not looking at you from the past and not even the present but waits for you as you surrender to him. Faith cannot be seen, and neither is God, but this experience will prove to be the abundant life. Actually, it is referred to as a new creature in Christ. (2 Corinthians 5:17-21).

Let your mind become renewed from this day forth. Remember, a renewed mind seeks the kingdom of God first daily (Matthew 6:33). You can always go to God the Father because you are in the family, and he will lead and guide you. Learn to listen to him; he will renew your mind, but he uses your heart to do so.

A personal request that I ask of you is found in Proverbs 3:5-6. **Trust in the Lord** with all your heart and lean not on your own understanding; in all your ways submit to him, and he will make your paths straight. You will soon come to know this to be true. Easier said than done, but the more this is done, the easier it will become.

Part III
A Hard Head But an Open Door

Of all the things that have happened in my life, the day that I was temporarily trapped underneath my van remains foremost. As a tyro mechanic, I was doing routine preventative maintenance on my vehicles at home. This Saturday afternoon I was determined to complete the final adjustments to the full-size Ford van. I make mention of the size because of what will follow. The vehicle was idling rough, and with my limited knowledge of auto mechanics, I crawled under the van and accidentally touched some link (I was told later it was the transmission), and the vehicle came out of gear and started to move backwards. To my surprise, my daughter was playing in the driveway at the rear of the van. Suddenly, I realized that I was trapped and was uncertain as to what to do. I was stunned and concerned if my child would be run over by the van. I never thought too much about how I was going to remove myself from underneath it. It all happened so quickly. It appeared that time had escaped me. How do I get from under the van and rescue my daughter? Thank God, I stopped the van and rescued my daughter before it rolled into the street. What and how I did it is still unbeknown to me. Strange as it might sound, the good part is only the side of my face was run over by the front tire. With the skin removed and in what seemed like a conscious shock, I actually felt very little pain. "Do not be afraid or discouraged, for the LORD will personally go ahead of you. He will be with you; he will neither fail you nor abandon you" (Deuteronomy 31:8). I had no clue what that meant at the time, but oh, how appreciative I am of that truth today. How true this scripture was and is! The words were so, so familiar. To reference these scriptures is one thing; when we experience them, they become certain. No longer is it what they (others) say, but I say, "But God."

Not aware of all that occurred, my wife and daughter informed me that my face imprint and hair were in the asphalt driveway. The phenomenal part of all of this is that there was a peace that came upon me like I had never experienced before. It was as if God raised me far above what had happened and allowed me to enter a mental state of thanksgiving. With an overwhelming feeling of thankfulness, I could not stop praising him. Of course, my family could not understand what was happening, and neither could I at first—then, "Peace I leave with you; my peace I give unto you; not as the world giveth, give I unto you. Let not your heart be troubled, neither let it be afraid" (John 14:27). Can you imagine, amid all that, that I had peace? I have learned and accepted that to get such peace, the mind must be renewed. I was beginning to understand that there was a place of peace beyond my understanding. What followed amazed everyone. My wife and I were to renew our wedding vows within 30 days. Within two weeks of the scheduled celebration, there was only a small mark on my face. That blemish has become an open door (testimony) for me. It's been said that God knows how to get our attention, and for me, this was just the beginning. Peace will chase distractions away. In this case, it was apparent that peace was greater than fear.

Part IV
Scattered Thoughts May Land Anywhere

We have so many premeditated thoughts that it seems impossible for our mind to be renewed. What an embarrassment as Christians when we have the mind of Christ. This might seem incomprehensible to say, but it is according to scripture.

1 Corinthians 2:16: For who hath known the mind of the Lord, that he may instruct him? But we have the mind of Christ. The Christ mind retains the thought of accomplishing the impossible. Matthew 21:22: And all things, whatsoever you shall ask in prayer, believing, you shall receive. To do so, we must seek him, but we must do so with all our hearts without wavering. One step at a time, it is a continued process. Don't compete; rather, repeat the process. Man looks at the outside, but God looks at the heart, and the pure in heart shall see God.

Let's look at additional Bible verses, which I hope will be helpful to you too.

Romans 12:2: And be not conformed to this world, but be ye transformed by the renewing of your mind, that ye may prove what [is] that good, acceptable, and perfect will of God. 1 Corinthians 2:14-16: But the natural man receiveth not the things of the Spirit of God, for they are foolishness unto him; neither can he know [them], because they are spiritually discerned.

Philippians 2:5: Let this mind be in you, which was also in Christ Jesus:

2 Timothy 1:7: For God hath not given us the spirit of fear, but of power, and of love, and of a sound mind. 1 Peter 4:17: For the time [is come] that judgment must begin at the house of God; and if [it] first [begin] at us, what shall the end [be] of them that obey not the gospel of God?

Ephesians 5:1: Be ye therefore followers of God, as dear

children; Romans 8:1-39: [There is] therefore now no condemnation to them, which are in Christ Jesus, who walk not after the flesh, but after the Spirit. Philippians 4:8: Finally, brethren, whatsoever things are true, whatsoever things [are] honest, whatsoever things [are] just, whatsoever things [are] pure, whatsoever things [are] lovely, whatsoever things [are] of good report; if [there be] any virtue and if [there be] any praise, think on these things. We spend time worrying about things that we cannot change or that we care not to change. "Speak to the mountain, and the mountain will move (Matthew 21:21)." Often we do so only to become disappointed and exhausted because of no movement. We ask why the mountain did not move. Maybe we are that little foothill that is speaking to a mountain. Could the problem be a lack of participation on our part or overlooking the need for a front-row view of ourselves? Self-enrollment in the blame game is very expensive and time-consuming. Faith is simple and simply applied when we accept our part. Rather than trusting God, not his timing, will cause us to make allowances for our impatience. God's timing is not restricted to our twenty-four-hour clock or time zone. Early or late time belongs to him.

Renewing of the mind is as necessary as sleeping, eating, and giving proper care to the natural man (the body/flesh). By the way, this is not just for a select few. It is for all that will submit, learn, listen, and obey the leading of the Almighty God.

Jesus was successful in his earthly ministry because he was always submissive to the will of God. When Jesus was confronted by the multitude, he healed them (Matt. 12:15), moved with compassion (Matt. 14:14), and always provided for their needs. Will he not today meet ours?

Yes, but we must learn to purposefully stay on track.

Once Jesus was confronted by the crowd (John 8:5), and their concerns were what Moses had said in the law, their self-righteousness, and what should be done to the woman in their midst. He replied, "He that is without sin cast a stone at her." Beware of fault-finding; God wants our minds to be renewed

Simply Faith

in every situation. I recommend reading the complete chapter.

But how do we renew our minds? Let's listen in on the question asked by Nicodemus (John 3:4). He wanted to know how a man could be born again. Nicodemus was a teacher—teaching what should have been common knowledge to him. You see, it does not matter if you are a preacher, Sunday school teacher, deacon, etc., in the church—what is important is becoming familiar with and renewing your mind on God's word. Becoming set free by the scriptures.

The Apostle Paul alerted us to this when he said, "Finally, brethren, whatever things are true, whatever things are honest, whatever things are just, whatever things are pure, whatever things are lovely, whatever things are of good report; if there be any virtue, and if there be any praise, think on these things." He further stated, "Those things which ye have learned, received, and heard, and seeing me, do, and the God of peace shall be with you. When we renew our mind in the Word, we gain peace of mind. We begin to understand what Jesus meant when he said, "Peace I leave with you; my peace I give unto you; not as the world giveth, give I unto you. Let not your heart be troubled, neither let it be afraid." Therefore, we must have an ear to hear and receive faith to be renewed in our minds to accept it. The good part about it is "God hath dealt to every man the measure of faith." If it is the size of a mustard seed, that will move mountains. So, watch you, stand fast in the faith, and walk by faith and not by sight. And such trust has been through Christ toward God. Not that we are sufficient of ourselves to think anything of ourselves, but our sufficiency is of God.

Guess what? He supplies all our needs. The first encounter with God's son Jesus is an open opportunity to push the refresh mental button and begin to renew our minds. Listen, "By grace (God's unmerited favor-time granted) are ye saved through faith." If any man will come after, Jesus said, I will in no wise cast him out. God is saying if a man, woman, boy, or girl, regardless of their past, would change his or her mind, that salvation is available to them. All that it takes to receive eternal life is a changed (renewed) mind. The Hebrew word for change is shanah, which means duplicate; therefore, when you hear and apply what was heard, it becomes the starting point for a fulfilled daily life.

The first man, Adam's fall, caused a domino effect on humanity; therefore, man had to be restored and renewed. Your mind will try to play all kinds of tricks on you, but we must be aware of the facts. That is, the inward man is renewed day by day, and we must be renewed in the spirit of your mind. Otherwise, it will be the outward man leading us to carnal things, causing us to perish. It's a daily renewing of the mind, not mind over matter.

Thank God, it is the Spirit that giveth life that enables us to discover the will of God and direction for our lives. And if any man be in Christ, that man becomes a new creature, and old things are passed away. Day-to-day we need to renew our minds to eliminate the old things. What is the solution to the many problems that we face in this life? Psalms 37 gives us a good example of how to stay renewed in the Spirit of your mind: "Trust in the Lord and do good... Delight thyself also in the Lord, and he shall give thee the desires of thine heart." The psalmist further says, "Rest in the Lord, and wait patiently for him... Cease from anger and forsake wrath; fret not thyself in any way to do evil." Nevertheless, we must commit our ways unto the Lord and trust in him, and he shall bring it to pass. What shall he bring to pass? The renewing of our mind through the word of God. The guarantee is that the steps of a (the believer) good man are ordered by the Lord, and he delighted in his way. Though he falls, he shall not be utterly cast down, for the Lord upholdeth him with his hand (Psalm 37:23-24). As we renew our minds, we come to realize that God honors his word. His word will never come short of its promises.

Renewing of the mind is necessary to replace what is old, worn, and exhausted, allowing us to start anew with a fresh supply, which is God's word. This transitional process will create in you a clean heart and open your eyes and heart. Renewing your mind will cause you to let go of the past. You will become aware of forgiving unconditionally, as often as necessary, and asking for forgiveness when you fail. You will accept apologies with joy and thankfulness, encourage and invite harmony, and remember your own imperfections when you relate to others. Store this in your heart and meditate on it. It will give birth to the new you. Let's pause for a moment. Are you beginning to see the need to accept the invitation mentioned above? At any time, feel free to do so. When you are ready to surrender, God is always waiting. It is not so much a feeling as a promise to be granted.

Fruit produces after its own kind. If your mind is being renewed day by day, you will change both positionally and spiritually. It's okay to recycle your negative into positive to help renew someone else. However, you must be equipped to say, "I know whom I have believed, and am persuaded that he is able to keep that which I have committed unto him against that day" (2 Timothy 1:12). Note: It does not say "I know in whom" but rather "I know whom I have believed." What makes the difference is knowing. If we are not sure or do not know, we can become doubtful and double-minded. We are told that if a man is double-minded, he cannot receive anything from the Lord. Why? Because he is unstable (James 4:8). What we learn here is the word of God is not bound (2 Timothy 2:9). If in doubt, let go and let God. He will never leave us—never. He becomes a permanent resident.

We must be renewed in the spirit of our minds as Christians. What does this entail? The Christian must be broken in spirit, burdened for others, meek, humble, hungry for righteousness, merciful, pure in heart, patient, loving, joyful, gracious, and kind. You don't have to go it alone. In time, this too shall become second nature. Remember, God's word will not come back void – we are never alone, lonely, but never alone. We must trust this to be so for it to be so. He keeps his promises. It is a transformation that I refer to as a renewing of the mind.

How are we going to accomplish this? To quote the Apostle Paul, "Casting down imagination and every high thing (thought) that exalted itself against the knowledge of God and bringing into captivity EVERY thought to the obedience of Christ. (2 Corinthians 10:5-7). We must make up our minds and become active participants. Otherwise, disobedience will become our adversary. But thank God, he has given us the Believers Enemy Amour Resource (BEAR). In Ephesians 6:10-18, we read, "Finally, my brethren, be strong in the Lord and in the power of his might. (not our might). Put on the whole armor (not part) of God, that ye may be able to stand against the wiles of the devil. SEE WHY OUR MINDS MUST BE RENEWED? So that we may be able to stand against the wiles of the devil. For we wrestle not against flesh and blood but against principalities, against powers, against the rulers of the darkness of this world, against spiritual wickedness in high places. Therefore, take unto you the whole armor of God, that ye may be able to withstand in the evil day, and having done all, to stand. STAND, therefore,

HAVING your loins girded about with truth, and HAVING on the breastplate of righteousness, and your feet shod with the preparation of the gospel of peace; above all, taking the shield of faith, with which ye shall be able to quench all the fiery darts of the wicked. And take the helmet of salvation and the sword of the Spirit, which is the word of God; Pray always with all prayer and supplication for all saints..." In time, the outfit will fit.

It is impossible to do this without your mind renewed. As I think about the above scripture, I personally am reminded of the many unnecessary hardships, abuses, fears, and shadows of death I traveled before my mind could accept the fact that God so loved me that he gave His ONLY son for me. Then and only then could I grasp the love of God—that love renewed and transformed my mind. Read for information and inspiration, and in time there will be illumination and revelation.

Simply Faith

The song I had heard in the past became a reality. "Amazing Grace, how sweet the sound that saved me." Lord, I was lost, but now I am found, which caused me to rejoice.

What a welcome awareness of promised possibilities. "As you have, therefore, received Christ Jesus the Lord, so walk you in him, rooted and built up in him, and established in the faith, as you have been taught, abounding with thanksgiving... And you are complete in him, who is the head of all principality and power. And have put on the new man, that is renewed in knowledge after the image of him that created him." And as the second chapter of the epistle of Timothy verse twenty-one states, "(purge yourself) ...he shall be a vessel unto honor...meet for the master's use and prepared unto every good work. This cannot be accomplished except we become fully persuaded. We see and have experienced the thought expressed in Galatians 1:10 by Paul when he said, "For do I now persuade men, or God?" He had ministered to Agrippa of all that had taken place in his contact with The Almighty God on the road to Damascus, and still King Agrippa was almost persuaded. It almost sounds good, but it is not good enough in desperate times. The heart channels the word to the mind. Paul was subjected to many distractions and insults. Festus said to him with a loud voice, Paul, thou are beside thyself; much learning doth make thee mad. Paul like you and I had to be convinced, believe, have confidence, content, obey, trust and yield. We are instructed to let every man be fully persuaded in his own mind is the suggestion Paul gives. We must learn not to be almost but persuaded. We must be fully persuaded.

There are many scripture references of those who were persuaded and renewed in their minds. As God was with these individuals, so shall he be with us. How can we be sure? Be persuaded; believe it: "He's the same yesterday, today, and forevermore." Let's take a trip through the scriptures to see what the record has to say about it.

There was Abraham, who is called the father of faith. He was a man who followed the leading of God without reservation. When Abraham was one hundred years old, Isaac was born (the son of promise). Happy that he and Sarah were to have this child; not long afterwards this same child is offered up to God for a sacrifice. The test of a servant was far greater than the test of a father for his son. God requested Abraham to place his son on the altar, and he willingly obeyed. The result was that God spared Isaac. Why? because Abraham believed God, and it was credited to him as righteousness. He must have had a mind that would trust God with ALL that he had and at ALL cost. Would you have done that? With a renewed mind, you would have. Think about it: everything belongs to God, why not trust Him with what belongs to Him, you, and me. Abraham was asked to offer his son Isaac. God freely gave His only begotten son, Jesus. Thank God for the lessons learned through their obedience.

In Genesis 50:24, we see a remarkable act of faith displayed in the life of Joseph. He was mistreated and abandoned by his family; rather than losing hope, his faith increased. He was not influenced by Egyptians, nor did it weaken his trust in God. Joseph Faith was firm. He did not let the opposition deter him; he knew what he believed and that, through faith, deliverance would become a reality. He was convinced that he might have been displaced in Egypt, but he knew where he belonged. For him the scripture truly applied: "Weeping endures for a night, but joy cometh in the morning" (Psalm 30:5). Being fully persuaded will enable us to have peace because of a transformed mind. As we come to know the God of the Bible, we begin to have the mind of Christ dutifully (1 Corinthians 2:16 and Romans 12:2).

This spiritual expedition might seem to have grueling terrain with many challenges but find comfort that we are not making the trip alone. As demanding and incomprehensible as it might appear initially, you will pass the test because God has all of the answers. Again, it will be grueling, but in the end, it will make you a better person as a result of it. A solid foundation is being established. We decrease to ourselves; we are to increase in the things of God. Just think: one day you will be sharing this learned lesson with others. Looking back over my life, this was not in my view either. Things were obscured; however, I now have a clearer understanding and have a better view of what's ahead.

There will always be questions, but there are basic things that must be addressed. Actually, there are some that need to be answered early on, like the ones to follow.

Part V
SELF-TEST

(1 Cor. 13:5)
Where do you stand spiritually?
Ask yourself the following questions:
    Who is God? Do I know who God is?
    Do I know how to get to know him?
    Do I want to talk with Him?
    Do I love God?
    Do I know that I can be or have been forgiven?
    Do I know how to pray?
    Do I know what love is?
    Do I know how to study the word of God?
    Am I a Christian?
    Do I know what a Christian is?
    Do I have Christian friends?
    Do I go to church?
    Do I really know what the church is?
    Who am I? Do I really know who I am?
    Do I have a reason for not submitting to God?
    BE HONEST WITH YOURSELF

Test results are based on an awareness of one's self and the need to make changes, which is far greater than the point system.

The devil always tells us we are not good enough. In John 10:10, the thief does not come except to steal, to kill, and to destroy. God says, I have come that they may have life, and that they may have it more abundantly. When the devil comes, remember, so does Jesus. Think about that for a moment; I don't have to go it alone, and he promises to never leave us. That's good news!

Never let the devil knock at your door and deliver a

package that does not belong to you. And never, never let him give you something that appears to be free. Good advice is if you did not order it, don't take it. Proverbs 3:13 "Happy is the man that findeth wisdom, and the man that gets understanding." God wants us to be happy, and what could be more satisfying than having a renewed mind? How do we get this? Remember that faith comes by hearing the word of God. This is vital because Jesus emphasized that man shall not live by bread alone but by every word of God (Matthew 4:4). Remember, worry will never change a thing, and procrastination will block the mind from doing anything. We can't have a renewed mind if we will not give God our concerns, problems, thoughts, and cares. Until we come to the place where we can say, "Let every man be fully persuaded in his own mind," then we will continue to be displaced spiritually (Romans 14:4).

Corrective action is necessary to believe God is true to His word. Therefore, we boldly go after the promises of God. We must reject fear, don't settle for mediocrity, and go beyond the decision-making process. DECIDE to take His word as final authority. Seek and learn to listen and to distinguish His voice. He speaks to us through His word. Practical application will prove this to be so.

An example of this was that of Joshua and Caleb, two of the twelve spies (Numbers 13:27, 28, 30-31), who had a positive report and saw things differently than the others.

Like these two, we get lots of opportunities to be negative and afraid, but we must press toward the mark of the prize of God. We must be renewed in the spirit of our minds (Eph. 4:23). The location may be the same, but those with a renewed mind will see things differently. And that difference can and will result in victory or defeat.

We hear in Christian circles, "Get into the word," and we should stay in the word. The question often asked is, How? To get into the word, you must have a taste, an appetite, and a hunger. No one can have faith in something that they are ignorant about. We must have ears to hear. When it comes, be ready to receive. It is hard to study where there is no interest, and you will not retain what you have not learned, if anything at all. As the Lord said to Joshua, "Meditate therein day and night, that thou mayest observe to do according to all that is written therein; for then thou shalt make thy way prosperous, and then thou shalt have good success." God also instructed him, Be strong and of good courage; be not afraid, neither be thou dismayed; for the Lord, thy God, is with thee wherever thou goest (Joshua 1:9). " Like Joshua, we are to be encouraged and to stay the course, and the result will be triumph. Until we hear the Lord, we cannot have the joy of the Lord. That is why we must remember that faith cometh by hearing (over and over). In the natural world, we would be swayed to believe that repetition means deficient or a slow learner, but not so with God and the scriptures. Hearing (over and over) the word of God, which comes through hearing, will strengthen us.

Think about this for a moment: the Christian is what Satan can NEVER be. We are heirs of God and joint heirs with Christ. An heir is a beneficiary or recipient of another. When we become transformed by the renewing of our mind as believers (Romans 12:2), we become members of the family, "heirs of God and co-heirs with Christ" (Romans 8:17). This is very important to know; otherwise, we will suffer from not being aware of who we are. What I refer to as an identity crisis. Worse is to have a false identity.

In Isaiah chapter 14:14-17 "I will ascend above the heights of the clouds; I will be like the most High." Satan wanted to be like the Most High and was disappointed that he could never be. Take hold of this truth: we are created in God's image and likeness. Let that sink in for a moment. We are created in the image and likeness of God. Equipped with that understanding will provide for us the doorway to appreciating all that Almighty God has done. Thus, it should not be difficult to communicate with God. Again, we are created in His image and likeness. I like calling it made a new. God expects, and we should converse with Him often, even before facing trouble and assuredly afterwards.

When we are made anew, our minds are also renewed. How so? Apostle Paul stated that "if any man be in Christ, he is a new creature: old things are passed away; behold, all things are become new. We become ambassadors (his representatives) on the earth. We may not realize it, but from God's point of view, we are, and we never will be the same. This should inspire you to alter your way of thinking. Seeing the new you as God sees you. Not recycled, but a new creature in Christ Jesus.

A scripture that assures me that God is ready to redeem us in Psalms 50:23 says, "Giving thanks is the sacrifice that honors me, and I will surely save all who obey me." When we obey Almighty God, it is the renewed mind that is in touch with the will of God for our lives. It is understanding the difference between free will, self-will, and God's will. When seeking the will of God, there must be a conscious effort to accept and obey.

If there was ever a time when this was to be, it was the day that I contacted a young teenager. He called and asked if I would come by and help start a lawn mower that he had a problem starting. It was Friday afternoon, and I had planned to meet someone else at my home plus several other engagements. Please note, these were my plans. Whose plans? Mine. Purpose and plans are not the same. On the way, stopped in the middle of the street, was a man whose car had run out of gas. Again, it is Friday afternoon in busy downtown. People were blowing the horn, yelling, and zooming by. It seems that things happen when they should not. I stopped to help, and he really needed assistance. You would not believe it, but the man did not have a can for gas, money, or his wallet. Strange as it might sound—and this is the good part—I only had twenty-five cents to jumpstart the teen's lawnmower. I was reminded that "my God shall supply..." but how with twenty-five cents? Well, I got out and began directing traffic.

After moving the car, I suggested that the driver wait until

I got back. This gave me time to pick up my young fellow, which I did. Guess what? He had a can of gasoline with gas in it and dollars to boot. What did God do? He did exactly what the word says: "He shall (and did) supply my need for the driver. How much money did I have? twenty-five cents. What joy it was to have the young friend with me. We put the gas in the car and a Bible tract in the man's hand and back to my plans. During the events to follow, I discovered that this young fellow needed talking to and really wanted me to be all ears to hear. He talked, and I listened, and vice versa. Then it was clear that we can only fulfill God's will and supply other's needs when we have the mind of Christ and the heart to obey. God's timing makes the difference every time. I was able to accomplish all that God had purposed. Oh, the young fellow was part of a youth group that I had assisted in getting a lawn care job for the summer. "Give and it shall be given" was on display. What a welcomed truth that had been proved to all parties. It all worked out according to God's plan.

It is more than I could have ever imagined writing this book. But one thing I have been assured of is that for me it was a must. How? I have met many people that were on the brink of quitting, giving up, running away, feeling displaced, overthinking, and hurting. When I would mention how I had fought with the challenge of this project, I was encouraged to "please do it." It has become a personal blessing because I have grappled with some of the same challenges myself. What a welcomed opportunity to reflect and to share. Our trials, surprisingly, can be encouragement to others.

Like the story of a lady who said that she had been raped and had never shared this information with anyone until that day. At the close of the workshop, she wanted to talk with the understanding that no names would be shared. The discussion was a challenge, but her request was respected. How important it was for the audience to be attentive to the freedom of her experience. As she dismounted her feelings, it was as though her mind was being renewed. There was nothing for her to be ashamed of; she was not at fault; she did not cause it to happen; yet, without reservation, personal forgiveness flowed from her lips. "I have never told anyone this" with a sense of relief or condemnation. When the mind is renewed, out goes the bad (at least room is made), and in comes the new. Can you imagine how many others are carrying around years of such weight?

In John 8:36, Jesus makes a wonderful statement of victory. He says, "So if the Son sets you free, you will be free indeed." Free means to be unrestricted, welcomed, uninhibited, and open. This freedom of change is not limitless and is emancipated. This can only happen when there is spiritual deliverance. It is a pardon that can only be understood and appreciated between you and God.

Other cases: Without going into detail, there are more–to name a few:

* The child that was screamed at repeatedly because she had difficulty reading in the first grade. To finally find a teacher who was patient with her until the screams turned into praise once delivered.

* The grown man with childlike feelings was rejected by his family. That is, until he met his biological father, who told him and expressed love for him. There was an instant change.

* The person who used drugs because he was told he was a failure. He was later tested to discover that he had an exceptional IQ and had been in a remedial setting during his early childhood.

* The person blamed God for a childhood injury (his cousin was killed). The guilt trip of the parents was placed on his shoulder. The truth freed him. He accepted the fact that he had nothing to do with it.

* The person who thought they were beyond being loved. No longer has to imagine if they can. Expressed love and acceptance by others paved the way.

* The child was rejected by her parents, resulting in her becoming a wayward youth. When rescued by the grandparents with so much love, the memories of the past vanished. The

mind is the human data bank. Data received by hearing is stored in the mind, which is our memory. We find in Romans 10:17 this truth. "So, then faith cometh by hearing." Just as faith cometh, so do doubt, prejudice, fear, unbelief, failures, etc. Therefore, the natural man's mind cannot receive the things of God. Why? Because they must be spiritually discerned. Until the individual is born again, meaning the acceptance of Jesus Christ through repentance, confession, and belief, we will not be able to alter this database. With the same old programs, we get the same old results. Yet, when we update our program (thinking/believing), we become renewed in the mind. Jesus said in a very familiar verse (John 3:16) that God gave His only begotten son, that whosoever believeth in him should not perish but should have everlasting life. Jesus talks about everlasting (never-ending) life. For most Christians, the thought of this truth must be rehearsed over and over. We too forget or make light of eternity and think only day-to-day. We see that the mind must continue to be renewed. This is not a one-time makeover. Like the little girl, until she heard differently, it was hard for her to believe differently.

So, don't let the stumbles of yesterday hinder your walk with God and your mind to be renewed. It is to refresh rather than a restart button.

The thief (Satan) comes to steal from you God's abundance. (John 10:10) Why? Because as a man thinks in his heart, so is he. Don't let it get into your heart. "Let not your heart be troubled" (John 14:1). Your heart is the ground for the seed of faith to grow the Word of God. If you want to be healthy, you must eat properly. Sweets in moderation may be good to the taste but will damage the body. We would not expect anyone to eat ice cream for every meal, especially for breakfast. So, it is with an unregenerate mind. Naturally, we do things, often without thought, expecting the best results. For this to happen, however, we must decrease so that there will be an increase (John 3:30). Today the English version of the Bible states it this way: "He must become more important, while I become less important." When this is done, less attention is given to our problem, and more attention is focused on God's ability. Then the renewed mind is changed from "I don't know... to 'I can do all things through Christ that strengthens me." How? It is not through mind over matter but through the "joy of the Lord," and that joy is strength. My personal observation is that you can determine an individual's strength by their joy. Do you think this has some credibility?

Part VI
MENTAL EXERCISE - THINK ON THESE THINGS
(PHIL. 4:6-8)

Don't worry about anything; instead, pray about everything; tell God your needs, and don't forget to thank Him for His answers. If you do this, you will experience God's peace, which is far more wonderful than the human mind can understand. His peace will keep your thoughts and your hearts quiet and at rest as you trust in Christ Jesus. And now, brothers, as I close this letter, let me say this one more thing: Fix your thoughts on what is true, good, and right.

Think about things that are pure and lovely, and dwell on the fine, good things in others. Think about all you can praise God for and be glad about."

When we read the instruction given in Joshua 1:8-9, we become familiar with what is required as followers of the Word of God. Let's read what is being stated: "Keep this Book of the Law always on your lips; meditate on it day and night so that you may be careful to do everything written in it. Then you will be prosperous and successful. Have I not commanded you? Be strong and courageous." This has to be part and parcel of God's plan for his followers daily. Like Joshua, this must become a daily focus to remain steadfast to God's mission for life. He must have been baffled, and so will we be if we look at ourselves instead of focusing on the promise. Keep in mind that when distracted, we drift into the mist of self-destruction. God has said, "I will never, never fail you nor forsake you." Therefore, we are to never give up because our inner strength in the Lord is growing every day. And if we are growing every day, then we are renewed day-to-day. Let's consider this fact: wherever the word of God is mentioned, He (God) is present. When we read, quote, think, proclaim, and hear the word of

Simply Faith

God, God is present. If He is present, then His power is present. Jesus himself said that where two or three are gathered together in his name, there he is in the midst. Where His word is, He is.

Did you know that the devil realizes this and trembles? If the devil trembles, let us assume and accept our responsibility. To conquer is when we use the word of God by faith, and our spirit man is ready to receive its reward. We have the mind of Christ, the word of God, and the power with us at all times. So, let us begin to use our weapons with certainty that God is here. It is necessary that we remember that He is here right now.

God said. Call unto me, hearken unto me, seek me, trust in me, delight yourself in me, and He will bless you exceedingly and abundantly. Don't you want God's best? If so, do not allow your mind to deny you of our promises. One promise is "ask and it shall be given you, followed by seek and ye shall find, and knock and the door shall be opened to you." God can be trusted.

What are we waiting for? Replace doubt and unbelief with the truth. God's word is true, and that truth will reward those who will believe. Let me make a point at this juncture; there will be problems, but there will always be God. Not a magic wand but a loving, all-knowing God that will love beyond the here and now.

Why is there so much talk about faith and yet so little result? I believe we discover the why in the Book of Romans, Chapter fourteen and verse twenty-two. Paul says to the Church at Rome, "Hast thou faith? Have {it} to thyself before God." What did the Apostle Paul mean? He was saying, Have it personally in the presence of God. Paul was saying, Keep your own conviction on the matter; keep it for your own comfort before God. If you are optimistic about a situation, you need never make a display of it. Remember what Paul said to the church initially in Romans 10:17? "So, then faith {cometh} by hearing and hearing by the word of God." Paul was reminding the church of what they should have known. That is to say, faith comes from the message, or must depend upon having heard the message, and the message comes from the reporter. The reported word is through the message of Christ or comes by the preaching of Christ.

While emphasis is placed on preaching, let it never be forgotten that the preaching of the gospel is not the exclusive responsibility of the clergy (Acts 8:4). Nor is preaching the exclusive means by which men may be saved. The written word, for example, is often an effective evangelistic tool. But in this context, Paul is emphasizing the report or message spoken by men of God. The word can never work until it is heard. Avoid blaming yourself for not knowing. You can't know what you don't know, but you can and must seek the truth. God is truth and willing and ready to share it with you. Make some time to be intimate with him.

Regarding hearing, we see in Romans 10:14, "How then shall they call on him in whom they have not believed? And how shall they believe in him of whom they haven't heard? And how shall they hear without a preacher?" Therefore, salvation does not occur apart from the Word of God. Let us look at additional scriptures: John 5:24 "Verily, verily, I say unto you, He that heareth my word and believeth on him that sent me hath everlasting life and shall not come into condemnation but is passed from death unto life." Acts 10:44 "While Peter yet spake these words, the Holy Ghost fell on all of them that heard the word." Ephesians 1:3 "Blessed be the God and Father of our Lord Jesus Christ, who has blessed us with all spiritual blessings in heavenly places in Christ." So, we see, with regard to believing, lost men cannot call without believing. Here is where faith enters in.

To receive this message of salvation requires faith. Much is being said and written about faith today. Yet, the truth is that faith comes from hearing the Word of God. The Word is the source of all true faith. The faith that the Word produces brings an awareness of God to the soul. By faith, the believer hears the voice of God as Adam and Eve did in the beginning. Faith, which the Word produces, enables the believer to exercise

Simply Faith

confidence in God and to believe Him for the impossible. Please note this impossibility is the norm for God, however.

The Word assures us that if we attune our ears to hear, our faith will be quickened (made alive), and God will work wondrous things on our behalf. And that is exactly what happened when I experienced the near-death accident on that Saturday. You see, the responsibility of man comes clearly into focus, but he must have first heard the word to apply it in every situation. The Word must be heard. The Word must be believed. That requires the listener to act in faith on the facts of the Word as presented. The Word clearly states, "No weapon that is formed against thee shall prosper, and every tongue that shall rise against thee in judgment thou shalt condemn.

This is the heritage of the servants of the Lord, and their righteousness is of me, saith the Lord."

Remember that words, thoughts, doubt, and unbelief can be weapons against faith. They are weapons of vain imagination. Put this in your mental toolbox: imagination is not real, but truth will withstand any obstacle.

Now we grasp why so little is accomplished; we don't really understand and operate in the faith that is ordained by God. Additionally, faith cannot and will not turn truth into a lie nor give ear to doubt. If this is your first encounter or if you have been walking with God for the greater part of your life, please keep in mind these words: temptation, yielding, and disobedience. These three words will always cause failure. Furthermore, they will produce temporary pleasure but deadly spiritual consequences.

Pride, on the other hand, will cause spiritual blindness, bondage, produce an evil heart (troubled heart), condemnation, and spiritual death or separation from God. We need to really understand faith's enemy, which is pride. Pride gives rise to misunderstanding; it disconnects the line of communication, it forfeits blessings, it manifests disrespect, and it will destroy anything in its path. It will break up marriages, families, churches, businesses, and friendships, and most hurtful is that pride will disrupt your relationship with God. It is commonly known as self-will, my way, the me and my, don't care, and well-known as the better you than me attitude. Its proof will never ask for forgiveness. Don't blame me is its reply.

"Just have faith." What does that mean? From the time we walked into the place of worship until the last person we met who professes to know God, we heard, "Have faith." Yes, we have heard this word seemingly all our lives. When we were very young, our "faith" was directed and determined by our peers and some authoritative adults. As we grew, we discovered another word used alongside "have faith." That word was to have pride. Actually, we were taught to have pride from childhood. Well, what are we to have, faith or pride? Which one has the upper hand over the other?

Let's take a more investigative approach. Faith in the Old Testament is more accurately rendered "faithfulness," indicating firmness, reliability, or steadfastness; the faithful individual holds on confidently to his own integrity and to the precepts of the Law, strengthened by his confidence in the object believed, the God of Israel. In the New Testament, faith is thought of as an act by which the individual avails himself of the gifts of God, submits himself in obedience to God's commands, and abandons all thought of self, trusting only in God. In other words, emphasis is not self-reliance but total God reliance. Paul to the Hebrews reveals his own learned behavior, that faith is always in opposition to sight; to him, faith is confident trust in the unseen power of God.

This is not the case with pride. Pride is the state of being proud or having inordinate self-esteem, conceit concerning one's talents, ability, wealth, station, etc., and disdainful behavior. Beginning with the story of the Fall in Gen. 3, pride is viewed as the root and essence of sin; it is seeking for oneself the honor and glory that properly belongs to God. A profound teaching on pride comes from the life and words of the Master (Jesus) himself. He condemned racial pride, the spiritual pride of the Pharisees, which manifested itself in ostentatious religious practices and other forms of social pride, while urging his disciples to assume an attitude of childlike humility. After all, Jesus said, "Except we come as a little child, we could not enter the kingdom." Thus faith, although it comes, will not work without the proper attitude toward God and intent of the individual. Jesus was the best example of his teaching ("he practices what he preached"), as seen in his washing the feet of the disciples and in his submission to death on the cross. Even at the cross, we see Jesus operating in faith.

He knew that his hour had come, but he also knew that his father would never leave him; that is why he echoed it to us, the body of believers, when he too said, "I will never leave you nor forsake you." Faith in God and trust in the Father is the combination that allows Jesus to not "take thought for tomorrow" because he knew that he was in the Father and the Father was in him. As believers, we need to come to grips with the fact that Jesus did not stop there. He also said, "I am in you." When does this take place? When you accepted Jesus as your sin-bearer, Saviour, and Lord of your life. Paul instructs us that the cross is the proper ground for Christian humility; apart from it, neither Jew nor Gentile has any grounds for boasting concerning his salvation, success, or accomplishments.

While the two are presented and received as being interchangeable, they are enemies. Faith will build you up, while pride will puff you up. Bodybuilders will tell you that exercising on a regular basis will build you up. Muscles will expand, and strength will increase. However, if we eat any and everything that we see, oh yeah, we will gain weight, but we will only be puffed up. We learn that as we exercise the word instead of our emotion, we will be built up in our inner part, which will light up our pathway in the world. When faith comes, we are equipped to "let your light (faith) shine," not shine your light (pride). Faith has the answer, but we must have a reason. Faith gives direction to a desire. Therefore, faith is the insight needed to light the path, lift the load, move the mountain, heal the body, and reward the believer.

When faith is in operation, the believer becomes knowledgeable of who he really is. When this knowledge starts to respond as a planted seed, we realize how powerful God is and how limited Satan is in power. "Behold, I give unto you power to tread on serpents and scorpions and over all the power of the enemy; and nothing shall by any means hurt you." (Luke 10:19). "And the God of peace shall bruise Satan under your feet shortly. The grace of our Lord Jesus Christ be with you. Amen." Faith in God's word will reveal to you that Satan is limited in his temptation." There hath no temptation taken you, but such is common to man; but God is faithful, who will not permit you to be tempted above that ye are able, but with the temptation, also make the way to escape, that ye may be able to bear it." (1 Cor. 10:13). Listen, Satan knows when he is defeated. James 4:7 says, "Submit yourselves, therefore, to God. Resist the devil, and he will flee from you." Faith cometh by hearing and hearing the word of God. God's word says, "Ye are of God, little children, and have overcome them because greater is he that is in you than he that is in the world." (1 John 4:4). Faith informs the believer that his mind must be renewed. Why? Because if any man be in Christ, he is a new creation; old things are passed away; behold, all things are become new." Before, you were a loser. But in Christ you are more than a conqueror.

But how can you be assured that you are a conqueror and that your mind is being renewed? Began to simply have faith in the word of God. Listen, John 15:7, "If you abide in me, and my words abide in you, you shall ask what you will, and it shall be done unto you." Who could know this better than the Apostle Paul? Paul's radical change becomes the experience of all born-again believers. Once dead, now they are alive. Formerly blind, they see! Christ makes new creations of those who believe, as real as God made Adam in the beginning. And remember, God does not have respect of person. And he is the same yesterday, today, and forever. Nevertheless, without faith, and He is the giver of that faith, it is impossible to please him. Think about it: God gives us faith to continue to become new from the inside out through a transformed mind and heart.

Biblical salvation not only brings something new, but it also subtracts something old. One's former set of values and his way of thinking disappear. His new outlook on life dictates a new lifestyle; the old becomes unworthy in his eyes. For he is no longer by his will or self-seeking desire but that which pleases God. He does not apply for credit but rather willingly gives God the credit due for the paid-in-full debt. By faith, through an experience as real as life, that allows us to be translated from the old person to the new.

We understand that **faith** cometh by hearing and hearing by the word of God (Rom. 10:17). Let's not be ignorant of the (enemy) **thief** (John 10:10) that cometh not, but for to steal (your faith) and to kill (your faith) and to destroy (your faith).

Part VII
But What Does This Really Mean?

A thief comes to steal means to take the property of another.
Come or go secretly, gradually, or unexpectedly.
To take away by force or unjust means
smuggle; to seize; without permission.
Win by trickery, skill, or daring.
To take another's possession without right and without his knowledge or permission.
Kill to deprive
To put an end to or stop,
consume, defeat, veto, slay, murder, assassinate.
Destroy to put out of existence
annihilate
cause destruction
demolish
to ruin the structure

Come to move toward something—with a specific purpose.
To advance toward accomplishment.
to appear on a scene
to happen, occur.

BUT Faith comes to the Rescue
Faith always arrives NOW and follows the request of that which is hoped for and leaves the evidence of things not seen. Make a mental note that faith is the evidence of things hoped for yet not gotten. Faith is never late by God's norms.

Part VIII
Determination vs. Faith

I will never forget the little girl that attended several of our services and was also in attendance at an open-air tent meeting. She was a very quiet young girl who got along with the other youngsters but was always very attentive to the teaching of the Word. As a matter of fact, during the open-air service she was so moved by the message that she responded to the call of God and was overwhelmed and anxious to apply what was said during the message. I was not aware that this little girl was having difficulties in school until I received a letter from her thanking me for the Word and saying she "wanted God to continue to watch over me and be blessed."

Here is the surprising yet good part of this story. That little girl had been in special education classes (for slow learners), but she was moved from that class and placed in regular classes due to her determination and application of faith that came by "hearing the word of God." She heard the word of God and applied it, and it resulted in the fulfillment of her desire. "What things so- ever you desire, when you pray, believe that you shall receive them, and you shall have them." This little girl desired to be in regular classes. She heard the word (it was not how much or how many times), and when she heard the word and applied the word (now faith), it produced a positive result. Why? Faith is always positive when it is God who communicates it and the receiver believes it and applies it.

Faith is the searchlight in darkness. It is the yes needed when you are surrounded with the answer no. It separates itself from the impossible. Faith is the arresting officer of conflict. It comforts a confused mind—gives stability to a hurting heart and a double mind. Faith always works for little pay (the size of a mustard seed). Faith never brags yet is always victorious. Does not have respect of person. (Ask the woman at the well, or the woman with the issue of blood, or even the Lord himself.) You'll be surprised at his immediate response. I believe it would be something like this: "Where I see faith, I stop to manifest its request."

A delay is not no!

We must learn that a delay is not a no! Think of faith as a seed that is put into the ground. During the waiting process, there is slow growth, but sooner or later, the sower is rewarded. Just as a pregnant woman must wait to give birth to the infant, so it is with faith. Remember, payday does not come before workday. You cannot see what you desire initially; there is a waiting period. Faith is not based on what you have; it is based on what is desired. We do not desire what we have. You may say I desire what I have, but you have it. At the most, you can appreciate it and be thankful, nevertheless, you still have it—it is not desired. So, it is with faith.

Faith looks in the direction in which we are looking. If there is faith, then there too will be a manifestation of its desire. Faith is a creative, producer, laborer, security guard, and a paymaster. The only assistance demanded to reward it is to believe it as truth with anticipation. What do you desire from God? Does it reflect faith? Does your faith waver, or are you drowning in doubt and unbelief? If it does, then your faith needs the assistance of a lifeguard. In him is life. Let his life-producing light brighten up your pathway so that you may become a receiving believer.

When I think of the discipline of faith, it reminds me of what is involved. Faith does not request intelligence—just obedience. Let's examine this thought more closely. Faith does not request an individual's intelligential qualification (it does not matter what his or her grade point average is) to determine the desire to be granted. How many people have you observed in life who had the potential to succeed in an area, and surprisingly enough, they did not? Often, we hear these replies, "That really was not for me." Even worse, "Anybody can do that; what's the use"?

Simply Faith

The person had the intelligence, the know-how, etc., yet intelligence was not the determining factor. For the sake of comparison, let's also look at the individual that was average in skill and knowledge yet applied their faith, determination, and steadfastness to succeed. Most of us would say, "That's the last person we would have ever thought would have made it." What made the difference? Was it the intelligent individual with the high IQ who took his ability for granted, or was it the individual with average skills who was persistent in his desire and application that thrived?

So, it is with you and me. If we have heard the word and not applied it to that which is desired based on the word, then failure will always be standing at the door. However, if we apply the Word and accept it as the final authority, then failure is defeated and success reigns. It is not how smart you are or how many scriptures you quote or the school that you may have attended. What is of most importance is your obedience to the word of God and the (self) assurance that what "He has said, He is also able to perform."

Attention!! Faith WARD March

Faith raises our hand in victory and not a hung head in defeat. Faith does not know its limits—it continues and continues and continues in pursuit until the mission is accomplished. Faith will never quit. You can manually turn it on, but once it starts, it switches into the automatic.

Faith does not doubt. Faith ignores past failures and welcomes the challenge of the opportunity to say yes to the present. Faith is obligated to keep its commitment, promise, and appointment. Faith is not moved or persuaded by failing. Faith will not ride in the back seat-it is the chauffeur for every believer. So, remember, simply faith is the faith that moves mountains, changes situations, renews relationships, encourages a broken heart, provides health to the sick, and provides fuel to the empty Christian in hope of the impossible. What's impossible with man is an opportunity with God.

My desire is that you complete this book with new hope.

May past disappointments and embarrassments become a testimony of stability. Hopefully, you will apply the word of God to alter situations and challenges in your life. It has been stated over and over, but I beseech you to always remember that faith comes by hearing and hearing and hearing and hearing the word of God. He will always be there to comfort your soul and listen to your cry. He wants us to know that "the righteous are not forsaken, nor will his seed (the believer) have to beg for bread." What do you need today?

Believe in spite of past disappointments, believe in spite of what has happened, believe in spite of past failures, and believe regardless of what doubt may say. Remember, the same God who said, "Let there be," awaits your request with anticipation that you and I need only to apply simple faith. For we are reminded that the believer is to walk by what he cannot see but believes without reservation that that same (whatever it is that he desires) will come to pass. Simply faith + trust + patience - doubt = the desired thing. Beware of the four "D's": doubt, delay, disappointment, and denial. It takes time to overcome habits and addictions. Trust the word of God to be true, and His word is the spiritual aid needed for mental stability.

WHY NOT FAITH?

What do you have to lose?

Little to nothing can be accomplished without it.

Faith is like fulfilling a goal.

Faith is like hitting a home run.

Faith is like scoring a touchdown.

Faith is like hitting the bull's-eye.

Faith requires both practice and patience-we have a responsibility; God has an obligation. Our responsibility is to have regard for God and His Word. We belong to God and can totally depend on Him. An awareness of this will transform our thinking with positive results. It is the beginning of a renewed mind. Imagine what goes through the mind of a child when they begin to walk. That first step, having feet and not knowing what to do with them? All they have is encouragement from

Simply Faith

their parents, grandparents, and other onlookers. "Come on, you can do it. Come on, do it for Mom, Dad, and especially the grands. They look at their audience in amazement when they take that first step. They pause, look at their little feet, but still, there are more to come. So, it is with us as we continue to hear the word of God. Faith comes by hearing, and assuredly, this is what is happening to us. God says, Come on, trust me, you can do it. Slow but sure until it is realized.

David was a shepherd boy, the youngest of his brothers and the son of Jesse. He tends sheep and learned a life lesson on how to have faith. His task was to care for and provide for the sheep and to protect them from harm and danger. This lesson of caring for the sheep and the responsibility associated with it led him to be confident. So much so that he was fearless when he encountered the giant. Keep in mind that this giant was feared by everyone. What kept David from being fearful? How was he able to defeat Goliath? David had talked with God. He trusted God, and God had never failed him. So, David had history, and this background experience assured him that again, God would provide. What did he do? He simply put into operation his God-given faith.

There was a story told of a young boy and how he had to go through the graveyard to get home. He would try to get home before dark because of the myth that had been told of events that happened at night. One day it was dark, and he was in the graveyard with this imagination running rampant. He could not walk fast enough, but suddenly he remembered the pastor preaching one Sunday on Whistling in the Dark. Somehow what he had heard during that church service calmed him as he rushed to get home. Reflecting on the message, he begins to drown out the imagination that otherwise would be a cause for fear. Anxious to get home, and in the middle of the graveyard, he started whistling. His takeaway from that experience was to let the word of God rule in your heart and mind. It worked for him, and assuredly it will for you and me. The greater the imagination, the louder he whistled. Make a mental note that sometimes we have to whistle in the dark.

God never asks, huh? He never says, Could you repeat that again? He is always listening with the understanding that we cannot receive without believing. Do we really believe that we can live and receive anything from God? Come on now–do we?

Blessed are those who **hunger and thirst** for righteousness, for they will be filled.

A lack of understanding and acceptance of the scriptures will result in spiritual malnourishment.

Faith is really a simple action that insists on surrendering to the word of God. This is evident in John 3:30, "I must decrease that He might increase." What's required is a change of attitude and a willingness to listen.

Jesus said, "Whatsoever things we desire, when we pray, believe that we receive them, and we shall have them." As I pondered these words, it was as if God were asking me, When you desire something, when do you want it? My immediate response was now. Therefore, I should pray for the desired result with the anticipation of receiving it now. I might have to wait, but my mind and heart desire it now. Expectancy now must be present. A test of my faith is manifested during the (trying) waiting period. No one desires to have what they want to show up in the distant future; we want it now. That's what the scripture means when it says faith is now, or it is not. It is now that prevents us from leaning on our own understanding. Let's take the Word of God as the final authority.

NOTE: Faith does not guarantee us that anything will happen. Faith does, however, assure us that we can and will be rescued from the doubt that hinders us. The assurance that we have faith is when we are tested. When we are tested, it will produce patience. Our ability and willingness in and during our experiences are introductions to patience that provide us the opportunity to trust the hand of God as He wills. Our faith is stretched as we begin to walk (step by step) by faith. In so doing, according to James chapter 1, we become perfect, complete, wanting nothing. Praise God! What a unique and

Simply Faith

profitable lesson to learn.

Be mindful of these words: faith, fact, fake, and feeling. They will show up with or without an invitation. We have to make the distinction and put them in their proper place. However, there is a word we seldom use, and yet it should be cherished. It is God's favor and thank God for it. Favor, by definition, is something done or granted out of goodwill rather than from justice or for remuneration; a kind act. This is what God does for us more often than we can imagine. Unknown to us, it helps us through the process.

JOSEPH - (Genesis Chapter 50) -as a youth, was assured that God had spoken to him and shared the vision with his family, which resulted in disappointment and quarrels Additionally, he suffered rejection, alienation, false accusation, and imprisonment. How was he to brave these confrontations? He remained God-inside-minded and purpose-driven. He knew that God was in the midst, and for that reason he could endure. Joseph concluded his experience, saying that what appeared to have been bad resulted in good. Why? Joseph was confident that God is almighty under all circumstances. His mind was renewed. Through it all, Joseph was able to say to his brothers, who meant him harm, and give an explanation as to why. "But as for you, ye thought evil against me, *but* God meant it for good." They were provided food during the famine. Faith provided a view far beyond their comprehension. They heard Joseph telling of his dream, but Joseph heard from God. In the end, what God told Joseph came to pass. God provided Joseph with the strength and protection to listen to Him. Even when false accusations were being made about him. In the process of renewing his mind, he witnessed greater and greater things in the end.

Faith does not have to be seen before it is believed. It follows God's lead until it reaches its destination. Faith is not swayed to believe in God only when things seem possible and is not moved in the least when things seem to go opposite to what has been asked. Faith reckons the impossible as possible.

Sight might be blurred initially, but the outcome will be clear.

Faith says to us to cease worrying about how and when God is going to do it. Permit God to run His own business in His own way and time. Faith the size of a grain of mustard seed allows us to say unto the mountain, Remove hence to yonder place, and it shall remove, and nothing shall be impossible unto you. Apparently, Joseph had that kind of conviction. He accepted what God said to be true and was committed to believing what He said. The dreamer's dream was fulfilled: he was blessed by God as promised. And all that was meant for evil against him, God meant it for good.

Story:

There was a **woman on board a ship** who was very afraid in a storm, but she saw her husband perfectly at peace, and she could not understand it. Her husband said he would tell her the reason, so snatching up a sword, he pointed it at her heart. She looked at it but did not tremble. "We'll," said he, "are you not afraid?" "No," she said, "because it is in your hands!"

"Ah!" he replied, "and that is why I am not afraid, because the storm is in my Father's hands, and he loves me better than I love you."

A **little child was at play** in a lower room, and as he played by himself, about every ten minutes he ran to the foot of the stairs and called out, "Mother, are you there?" and his mother answered, "Yes, I am here," and the little boy went back to play and was happy, as happy as could be, until again it crossed his mind that his mother might have gone. So, he ran to the stairs again and called, "Mother, are you there?" "All right," she said, and as he heard her voice again, he went once more to his play.

It's the same with us. In times of temporal trouble, we go to the mercy seat in prayer and say, Father, art thou there? As soon as you hear the voice that says, "It is I," you are no longer afraid. Your inner voice and mind bring peace to the heart that He is here. His presence makes all the difference.

Faith in action is when we are afraid in this way, yet we trust in the Lord.

Simply Faith

You may lack worldly possessions, status, or the applause of society and feel like something is missing. Let there be no uncertainty; God is willing, able, and ready to free you of anything that has held you captive in exchange for His peace.

When a person in captivity is freed instantly, there is a door to a new beginning.

Faith in Action– (the past has passed) Yet while we were sinners, Christ died for the ungodly.

What a lesson to be learned.

Faith is confident obedience to God's Word without apprehensions.

Faith operates quite simply. God speaks, and we hear His Word. We trust His Word and act on it no matter what the situations are or what the end result may be.

The circumstances may appear to be impossible, the consequences frightening, and unknown; but as we obey God's Word, we will discover that what awaits us is what is both right and is best.

Faith is only as good as its object, and the object of our faith is God. It is our total response to what God has revealed in His Word. We must be confident that what He has promised, He will perform. We cannot proceed without such conviction that the word of God is true.

Faith makes it possible for us to grasp what God does. Faith allows us to see what other folks cannot see. Faith authorizes us to do what others dare not do.

Mouth-to-mouth resuscitation is the act of assisting a victim or someone who has stopped breathing. So, it is with faith; it is the emergency assistance necessary when we are in a difficult and lifeless state. It is the second wind in the race that causes us to finish even if we do not win. Faith pushes us ahead, looking over the shoulder but never stopping and looking back. The challenge may be difficult, but faith says run, run, run; you can do it and you do. Time may be pressing, the mind may be thinking, people may be saying, but faith says only listen to me.

It entails providing air for a person who is not breathing or is not making sufficient respiratory effort on their own. So too, does faith aid the hearing when there is confrontation? It enables us to muster effort to avoid defeat. Faith does not guarantee you that nothing will happen but will rescue you if something does.

What advantage would we have if we committed to God in advance? If we did, we would have an alarm that would alert us to let go and let God instantaneously.

We hear a lot of things, and many are not true, but we still hear them. Many we accept as true; still, that does not make it so. Faith comes by hearing and hearing the word of God. So does untruth, and we need to distinguish the two so that we will have insight into God's plan for man. Remember, we shall know the truth, and the truth will make us free. Hearing the word of God will liberate us: faith will bring freedom. Therefore, when hearing, we must be sure that it is God that we are hearing. Otherwise, we will be listening to a stranger. A stranger is someone we don't know. We shall know the truth…truth is the pathway to freedom.

Faith is continuous hearing but believing must know the difference. Faith is not based on formulas, philosophies, theories, etc. Faith is based on believing the word of God.

The reason why we can believe is because God has given us faith, and faith insists on us doing so. Can you imagine going grocery shopping with no bag to put the items in? Comparatively speaking, God has provided us with the wherewithal to make good on his promises to us, yet we do not properly obtain them due to questionable faith. We must continue to hope for that which has been granted. Can you imagine a parent not fulfilling a request from their child or children? How much more difficult it is for God to keep his promise when we doubt him.

Faith without hope is uncertainty. If there is no destination, there will be no purpose. It becomes a struggle. Faith enables us to dress for battle with the understanding that we are limited but God has the provision for the vision. Otherwise, we will be limited and restricted in fighting the good fight of faith. Let's remember that the battle is not ours but the Lord's. In times of battle, it is our faith that is the warranty that God has everything under control. The great victory starts with taking God at his word. It's childlike faith in God and taking what He has said is true today, tomorrow, and forever. Neither circumstance nor situation should deter us from believing in God. What are our options, anyway?

Faith provides us with a position and posture that are steadfast and unmovable. It is a place of freedom and liberty despite confrontation. While it may take many years to experience this, it happens when we first believe. Our lack of knowledge does not mean that we have not been afforded it. You may be reading this from a prison or hospital: you may feel foolish–but God has chosen the foolish things to confound the wise. When we did not have a clue, God did. What he allows now, is time, time that is beginning to make sense. Walking by faith, you may experience a feeling of failure, but stay the course and discover that this is only temporary. Keep hearing, and your so-called failure will be a testimony of God's greatness. Remember, your eyes may fool you and your thinking might be challenged, but the word of God will stand forever. God does not have favorites, but we are indeed special to him. Faith is not an incident or experience or a temporary fix, nor an emotional rush, but rather the living extension of God in the heart and mind of the believer. It is walking in the presence of God continually. As I often ask God, how am I doing? Should I make a U-turn, put it in reverse, speed up, or slow down? Occasionally, he reminds me to be anxious about nothing. He has even told me to be still and know that He is God. In my quest to get closer to him, I am reminded that to do so, I must take him at his word daily. A gentle reminder: faith is not a one-time experience–it is a daily walk with Him. He is our lifeguard, and help is on the way.

Hold fast to this gentle reminder to the end. God promised

us that he would never leave us; therefore, we should walk in the reality of His presence. With that in mind, it will not work if there is sin. If there is unforgiveness, it will not work. (Psalms 66:18) He will not regard and answer my prayer. If there is pride, untruth, half-truths, and little white lies, faith will not work. Where sin abounds; grace much more abounds, but to him who knows to do it and does it not is sin. Sin takes flight and life out of the equation. The total of our effort becomes nothingness. In the eyes of man, you might be a flop, but God promotes you based on the intent of your heart. (Things God hates) You just might be surprised. Knowledge is power, and I want you to have this information to prevent you from failure. Proverbs 6:16-19 says, There are six things the Lord hates, seven that are detestable to him: haughty eyes, a lying tongue, hands that shed innocent blood, a heart that devises wicked schemes, feet that are quick to rush into evil, a false witness who pours out lies, and a person who stirs up conflict in the community. Psalm 11:5 The Lord examines the righteous, but the wicked, those who love violence, he hates with a passion.

However, John 3:16, 17 For God so loved the world that he gave his one and only Son that whoever believes in him shall not perish but have eternal life. For God did not send His Son into the world to condemn the world, but that the world through Him might be saved. Let's say we are believing and expecting God to do something for us. What is expected of us is to hope without doubt. We look forward to seeing what we are believing until it is manifested. Hope must be steadfast until faith becomes NOW. Keep in mind that biblical faith by definition is now faith. It must remain present, in the forefront, nearest and dearest. That means no doubt, no worry, and only expectation. It is challenging in the natural but has insight, and we can view it from afar. While we are waiting, "NOW" is illuminating. Faith is calling things that are not as though they were. Faith says you don't have to see it to believe it. It is the other way around: you must believe it before you see it. When we know the truth, the guessing game is over. When we realize

Simply Faith

the importance of "NOW," as is required in Hebrews 11:1, then our foundation becomes the starting point for answers. Simply applying faith does not mean that we will get what we want when we want it. Rather, the question is: Does what we want please God? Faith is the substance of things hoped for and the evidence of things not seen. God has dealt to every man the measure of faith. And we now know that "be it unto us according to our faith." It is a must that we understand that without faith (given to us by God), it is impossible to please Him. What that means is that the faith given to us is for the pleasure of God. This insight into God's plan will better help us to make a distinction between God's will and our intention. Good intention, apart from God's purpose, will result in confusion. And God is not the author of confusion. What then should be our focus? Apparently, the same as Jesus, "Not my will but your will be done." We are instructed to seek God first (Matthew 6:33). Many times, we desire to have all these things added without seeking him first, and, sad to say, often not at all. What an eye and heart-opener. We should seek to know if our will is God's will. If our desires correspond with His. Do we ask for God's input prior to decision-making? What is this about? Would it not be disrespectful to not get permission from our parents or those in authority before advancing our intention? Simply put, would you not request time off from your employer before doing so? Would you not alert your lending institution that your payment will be late? Better still, would you assume that it is okay to use a friend's credit card without permission? Why then should we not get God's say-so first? It is a matter of reverence, and surely we ought to do that.

This approach will reveal that His ways are not like ours more often than not. Waiting on Him should become natural to us. Why? Time belongs to him. He created all of this. To reference an old adage, "He may not come when we want Him, "but He's always on time." Wait, and you will see the reward of active faith. A very important step in the process is overlooked in the need for repentance. Repentance is like saying, "I am sorry; please forgive me." Think how little we hear such words; almost never today.

Remorse has to come before faith can come. The manifestation, freedom, and mountain-moving occurrence will and cannot happen until repentance has been activated. 1st things 1st: "Be it unto you according to your faith. We must believe it is that God can and will grant it.

The greatest experience in this life is the realization of faith. It is having confidence in God for things not seen. We can't see God, but faith gives us insight into the interworking of His purpose. Regardless of what is going on, He is in the midst. He has the final say so. Keep in mind that he can be heard even in silence.

Faith gives stability and brings reality within our grasp. An example that comes to mind is the lady whose son was gunned down who said, I thank God for the time we shared. What a challenging reality.

What seems often a teachable moment is the lady dying of cancer responded, "I have had a good time here, and now I prepare for the transition." And my late mother who would say, 'I will live while I can and die when I cannot help it'. My grandmother, before departing this earth, said, Lord, come see about me. The pastor, who had two bouts with death, said, God is in it. Wow!

How many times have you heard, "I don't believe He brought me this far to leave me?" Simply faith will not leave us in a time of despair. What an amazing discovery that God has given us with faith for all occasions.

I could mention the many encounters I have faced; even so, I am writing this book to express how grateful I am to God and hopefully encourage you to stay the course. Let's concentrate on God's promises and provisions even in adversities.

Thinking of giving up, finding it difficult to go through, throwing in the towel, or committing suicide? Maybe you feel like nobody cares or will understand. I beg you to starve that thought to death. Don't do it. Pause and mute yourself and ask

Simply Faith

what will be accomplished; seek peace instead.

Think about it and ask the question: What will be the outcome of the pain and the irrational decision? You may be scared with no one to talk to or listen to. This could be your now moment that seems impossible to resolve, but God will make it known. I believe that your conversation with him will, for as long as you want, produce a different and better outcome. As strange as it might seem, try it. He wants to hear what's on your heart. Go ahead, try for yourself, and see.

My mother would remind me that she would love me till the day she died. She did die, and I have learned that God will never leave nor forsake me. Let us not think that we understand what God has planned. God is not limited to what is happening now.

I have been writing this book for many years, and finally, I understand that the delay was for me to live it before I could share it with you. There is much more that I have learned since the beginning of this manuscript. What I have learned and am still learning is that God's desire for us as we continue this journey is to apply Simply Faith.

There will be many reasons to doubt, but our focus should be to believe the promise that God really cares. Faith in God can be compared to a 911 call that never hangs up—there is always an open line. God is listening, waiting, and He really does care.

Compassion is not feeling sorry but sharing the despondency. That is what God does with our quest for answers and comfort. He has the answers to the whys, how comes, and why me. Thank God he waits for us without a cutoff point. He's always waiting with open arms.

Yesterday, good or bad, there was a lesson to be learned, and it became a part of our history.

For with God, nothing shall be impossible, and because of God's love expressed through his only begotten Son, we can rest in the truth. Faith will allow you to have your greatest comeback. It is not magic—it is real. Faith could be called the

6th sense. The journey is attainable with help, and who could be more dependable than God? He is more familiar with this world than anyone we could think of. People with good intentions are only contributors, but He is the Creator.

Faith in God will not let you quit. You will not hit the target every time but believing that God is more than enough will provide another opportunity. If not, something else. God has a plan for your life, and it will surprise you that it is different from yours. Understand that—that's okay.

Remember that we need His strength to get things done. Take a deep breath of truth and allow this reality to take root. Don't waste time on yesterday's mistakes or hinder yourself from today's probability. Critique, but don't be overly critical of yourself.

There is something that we were told at a very young age, and we should not have forgotten. It was to listen to your inner self, and in doing so, you block out the loud sounds outside. Stop doubting yourself; God believes in you. It is not how long you live but what you do with your life. A mistake or seemingly wasted time just might prove that God has a different purpose for your life. We need to find out what it is. Refuse to see your time as a waste of time. When we discover what the purpose is, we will discover that it comes with goals. Your aspirations might appear to be unattainable, but God will help you reach them. Faith gives us an optimistic spirit that enables us to do it. Faith will clear the fog so that we will have a clearer view. It will bring calm to the turbulent thoughts while becoming the tag team partner and peace in seemingly difficult situations. Faith gently reminds us that we can become the role models of His promises. Don't be afraid to let God have his way in your life. He can be trusted, honestly. So, let us not let fear rob us of God's opportunity. Yes, we might be outmatched, but He is not. Get still before Him, wait, and He will reveal. Time with him is never unfruitful.

We would think the simple things would be the easiest. It seems to be so when it is not us.

Simply Faith

Learning to ride a bike, skate, or do public speaking could be included. But it takes time for that to become our reality. Although faith comes by hearing, we might not get it initially. Can you imagine the disappointment of not trusting God or waiting for the manifestation of our request.

Faith says, Why ask if you do not expect to receive? Is it a waste of time? Faith is not a technique but a process of building confidence and trust that will become unmovable when believed and applied. Faith in God is not trick or treat; it is a blessed promise to believers.

Locks operate differently. Some locks are open according to time, keys, and combinations, by hand or eye clearances. So, it is with faith: there are combinations required that often go unrecognized. In Matthew 7, Jesus said, "Ask and it shall be given." Yet, we spend much of our time trying to receive when He says to everyone that asks will receive. We ask and don't seem to get what is asked. Why? James 4:2 3 says we have not because we ask not. It is so easy to say, but what seems to be the hindrance? Let us inquire further; James 1:6 also says, "You must ask in faith, nothing wavering, for he that wavered is like the wave on the sea." This will be a life challenge to alert us that we should not be double-minded. Stay with me. Jesus said to ask and to not just say words but to believe those words. Oftentimes, we are desperate to pursue the promises of God rather than God. We should be honest with ourselves and truthful with God. If we need a little help, pray to be sincere and committed to the request.

Faith looks to the future, for that is where the greatest rewards are found. It is one thing to be in a den of lions, but what is so impressive is that Daniel did not focus on the lions. His sight was on God. Another gentle reminder: faith is the substance of things hoped for and the evidence of things not seen. It requires a commitment and undivided attention with God. Let us remember to not be distracted. It is not a luxury for a few "elite saints." It is a necessity for all who will trust God. Remember it's not as hard as you may think. It is actually taking God's word as a promise to you. Really? Really. Faith is possible to believers in all kinds of situations. Those who are in captivity can be freed, and you today too can be freed by faith. How? by hearing and becoming a doer of the word of God.

God always rewards true faith—if not immediately, ultimately.

Faith brings us out, takes us through, and brings us in. The requirement is that it is the size of a mustard seed. It doesn't take much—you don't have to be smart—just obedient.

Confinement of any kind will take over the mind. Free the mind, and the soul will be free.

Faith is never too late. You just wait and see. Fear is faith's enemy; faith makes dreams reality.

In spite of what it looks like, it is a confident assurance that something we want is going to happen. It is the certainty that what we hope for is waiting for us, even though we cannot see it up ahead. Our ears must be attentive. "Faith comes from hearing the message, and the message is heard through the Word of God." Romans 10:17.

Keep in mind that nothing will encourage you more than absolute faithfulness to God. He will see you through it all and remain sovereign overall. Having faith in God will provide you comfort when you are facing the unknown. Most importantly, his love never fails. The closer the relationship, the better our understanding of God. Time with God is not a waste but revealing.

God has dealt to every man the measure of faith, and for that reason the believer should always be in hope of things not seen. I want to caution you that faith does not say what will or will not happen, but it can and will alter the outcome. The notion that I or we can tell God what to do is disrespectful. It reveals the core of our understanding and reverence for who God is and who we are? A gentle reminder is that we are his sheep, and He is the shepherd. He leads, and we follow. Therefore, we should gain a balanced knowledge that His ways

Simply Faith

are not like ours. His being and ending just might not be as we perceive them to be. What an illustration of this when he prays and asks that the disciples watch. "You watch while I pray." That was not much to ask because praying was the most challenging part. They fail to watch for one hour. Today he is still asking us to watch and do the same. He prays to the Father, and now we pray to the Father in Jesus name. His prayer agreed with God, and so should ours. Faith in God allows us to focus on what truly is most important. What is most important is that we please God. Looking at what Jesus endured seems the opposite of his initial request.

Jesus was sent to this world to awaken us to the truth. So, let us not be disappointed when things do not go according to our plan but rather according to his will. Our main focus is to ask, seek, and knock until we are aware of and acknowledge His will. Until we accept the fact that life does have an end. As it is written, "It is appointed unto men once to die, and after that the judgment." Until we do, this will stifle and complicate living rather than mere existence.

What comes to mind is the nurse who said that her husband left for work and died at lunch tossing a Frisbee. "He was supposedly in good health, and his medical record stated that his heart just stopped beating."

The wife whose husband died at work after having a very pleasant phone call. "See you when you get home, which did not happen. She stated, "I have made it because God has allowed me to make it." What bothers me, however, is the death of family and friends, which causes me to have flashbacks." The ninety-five-year old widow who told of how her husband, at the age of forty-three, came home from work and worked in the yard while she prepared for dinner. Shortly afterward, he came and laid down to rest. When she called for him to come and eat, she discovered that he was dead. In that short span of time, he was gone. She would often say, "My love for him remained, and I never remarried." Not because she could not, but because she chose not to. With a smile on her face and a glow in her eyes, she said, How I longed for us to spend many years together. We did not, but I cherish the time we had together.

The mother whose son lay dead in the street after being gunned down. The hardest part was not being able to even touch him because of the crime tape, she said.

Mrs. Betty Lou was raised on a farm whose family were sharecroppers. Early on in life, he had to walk a great distance in hope of securing a basic education.

Unfortunately, after marrying the love of her life, he died in 2006. Determined to care for her family, she continued to work two jobs.

Her so-called real job was when she was promoted from the kitchen to drive-thru cashier.

While adjusting to the new job, her employer came behind her, touched her inappropriately, and said, You are doing a really good job.

As she said, "I felt like a fearful pauper talking to the King. Nonetheless, she told him never to touch her ever again. As a Christian employee, she can work but not compromise who she is. Since that time the owner, his sons, and his wife have died, yet she has remained employed by the new management to date.

She felt compelled to share how she encouraged a coworker to get his driver's license who walked for miles to work. This quest was a result of days that she walked and paddled a bicycle to work. You see, her son told her that if she would get her license, he would get her a car. Overwhelmed by the fulfillment of the promise, she wanted the same for her coworker. He has yet to get his license, but her son bought a bike for the employee. Furthermore, her son is in the process of making her dream come true for the coworker by buying her another car, and you guessed right, her car for the coworker.

While waiting for my order, she said that she has a neighbor who watched for her until she returned home safely at the end of the workday.

Simply Faith

I was told recently that she is retired and living a fulfilled life. She attributes all of her yesterday's victories to simply having faith in God.

Every one of them said that they had faith and still do. Nevertheless, what has allowed them to carry on has had the same response: "But God." I suppose God was guiding them with his eyes.

As we draw to a close, let's recapture some points of view with an open-minded methodology. Faith is much more than words spoken. Yes, God has dealt to every man the measure of faith, and that faith will be tested. We must avoid becoming double-minded and not asking amiss. That is to ask in faith, not wavering. Of course, this is not possible without an understanding and acceptance that the battle is not ours but the Lord's. Therefore, we must submit to God and resist the devil. Remember, faith is between you and God. It does not matter how many or how few people are involved; still, it equates to you and God. Not to sound superficial or cliché but having God on your side will insulate you from the onslaughts of life.

The disciples came to Jesus asking how they should pray. He shared with them what to do and say. God is always attentive. Jesus told us to have faith in God; let me say that again, Jesus the Son of God said, "Have faith in God." He was saying, Let nothing distract you; stay focused. That is what He did on the cross. Remember, "Not my will, but thy will be done"? He also said, "Father, I know that you always hear me." What a climax! What encouragement, knowing that God is always listening and waiting for us. Therefore, we can seek Him first, inquiring as to His will and allowing His will to be done. We can agree that waiting is one of the most difficult disciplines of life. In spite of everything, faith will enable us to wait for the fulfillment of God's purposes in God's time.

Let's be willing to trust His arrangement to be sufficient. "Wait on the Lord and be of good courage, and he shall strengthen your heart." Simple as it might sound, this is **simply faith.**

Linwood Best

Simply Faith

Toolbox for Spiritual Development

God said to Joshua 1:8 This book of the law shall not depart out of thy mouth, but thou shalt meditate therein day and night, that thou mayest observe to do according to all that is written therein; for then thou shalt make thy way prosperous, and then thou shalt have good success.

I have selected biblical references that will prove to be beneficial. As you read, study, and meditate upon them, you will develop a closer relationship with God and build a solid foundation

My hope is that you will be encouraged and grow in the knowledge of the scriptures.

Like Joshua, our ways will be prosperous, and we will have good success.

This is done through daily meditation and is achieved by being still before God in prayer.

I pray that this will become the doorway and scriptures to help to build your solid foundation.

Turning Water Into Wine, John 2:1-11
Healing the nobleman's son, John 4:46-54
The large catch of fish, Luke 5:1-11
Casting out an unclean spirit, Luke 4:33-37
Healing Peter's mother-in-law, Luke 4:38-39
Healing of a Leper, Luke 5:12-14
Healing the paralytic, Luke 5:17-26
Healing the man at the pool, John 5:1-16

Here we find a man at this pool who had visited this place often. He knew, like others, that at a certain time there was a moving of the water (a time to get healed), until now not him. After thirty-eight years of waiting, he could have just been going through the motions; that either way is okay. But on this day Jesus asked the impotent man, "Will you be made whole?" A simple act of faith is all that was needed.

Healing a man's withered hand, Luke 6:6-11
Healing the Centurion's servant of paralysis, Luke 7:1-10
Raising a widow's son, Luke 7:11-17
Healing the blind man and dumb demoniac man, Matthew 9:27-34
Still the storm, Luke 8:22-25
Healing the Gadarene demoniac, Luke 8:26-39
Raising Jairus' daughter, Luke 8:40-56
Healing the hemorrhaging woman, Luke 8:43-48
Feeding the five thousand, Luke 9:10-17
Walking on the Sea, John 6:16-21
Healing the Syrophoenician woman's daughter, Mark 7:24-30
Healing the multitudes and a deaf and dumb man, Mark 7:31-37

Psalm 23:1-6 ESV

A Psalm of David. The LORD is my shepherd; I shall not want. He makes me lie down in green pastures. He leads me beside still waters. He restores my soul. He leads me in paths of righteousness for his name's sake. Even though I walk through the valley of the shadow of death, I will fear no evil, for you are with me; your rod and your staff comfort me. You prepare a table before me in the presence of my enemies; you anoint my head with oil; my cup overflows. Philippians 4:6 ESV

Do not be anxious about anything, but in everything, by prayer and supplication with thanksgiving. let your requests be made known to God.

Isaiah 41:10-13 ESV

Fear not, for I am with you; be not dismayed, for I am your God; I will strengthen you, I will help you, I will uphold you with my righteous right hand. Behold, all who are incensed against you shall be put to shame and confounded; those who strive against you shall be as nothing and shall perish. You shall seek those who contend with you, but you shall not find them; those who war against you shall be as nothing at all. For I, the LORD your God, hold your right hand; it is I who say to you, "Fear not; I am the one who helps you."

Psalm 91:1-16 ESV

He who dwells in the shelter of the Most High will abide in the shadow of the Almighty. I will say to the LORD, "My refuge and my fortress, my God, in whom I trust." For he will deliver you from the snare of the fowler and from the deadly pestilence. He will cover you with his pinions, and under his wings you will find refuge; his faithfulness is a shield and buckler. You will not fear the terror of the night, nor the arrow that flies by day.

For thus said the Lord GOD, the Holy One of Israel, "In returning and rest you shall be saved; in quietness and in trust shall be your strength." But you were unwilling. Be angry, and do not sin; ponder in your own hearts on your beds and be silent. Selah

Romans 12:12 ESV

Rejoice in hope, be patient in tribulation, and be constant in prayer.

Isaiah 40:31 ESV

But they who wait for the LORD shall renew their strength; they shall mount up with wings like eagles; they shall run and not be weary; they shall walk and not faint.

Psalm 100:3 ESV

Know that the LORD, he is God! It is he who made us, and we are his; we are his people and the sheep of his pasture.

Romans 12:2 ESV

Do not be conformed to this world, but be transformed by the renewal of your mind, that by testing you may discern what is the will of God, what is good and acceptable and perfect.

2 Timothy 3:16 ESV

All Scripture is breathed out by God and profitable for teaching, for reproof, for correction, and for training in righteousness...

Psalm 27:14 ESV

Wait for the LORD; be strong, and let your heart take courage; wait for the LORD!

Luke 8:23-25 ESV

And as they sailed, he fell asleep. And a windstorm came down on the lake, and they were filling with water and were in danger. And they went and woke him, saying, "Master, Master, we are perishing!" And he awoke and rebuked the wind and the raging waves, and they ceased, and there was a calm. He said to them, "Where is your faith?" And they were afraid, and they marveled, saying to one another, "Who then is this, that he commands even winds and water, and they obey him?"

Mark 4:37-41 ESV

And a great windstorm arose, and the waves were breaking into the boat, so that the boat was already filling. But he was in the stern, asleep on the cushion. And they woke him and said to him, "Teacher, do you not care that we are perishing?" And he awoke and rebuked the wind and said to the sea, "Peace! Be still!" And the wind ceased, and there was a great calm. He said to them, "Why are you so afraid? Have you still no faith?" And they were filled with great fear and said to one another, "Who then is this, that even the wind and the sea obey him?"

Matthew 4:1-25 ESV

Then Jesus was led up by the Spirit into the wilderness to be tempted by the devil. And after fasting forty days and forty nights, he was hungry. And the tempter came and said to him, "If you are the Son of God, command these stones to become loaves of bread." But he answered, "It is written, "'Man shall not live by bread alone, but by every word that comes from the mouth of God.'" Then the devil took him to the holy city and set him on the pinnacle of the temple ...

Psalm 23:4 ESV

Even though I walk through the valley of the shadow of death, I will fear no evil, for you are with me; your rod and your staff, they comfort me.

Matthew 8:23-27 ESV

And when he got into the boat, his disciples followed him. And behold, there arose a great storm on the sea, so that the boat was being swamped by the waves; but he was asleep. And

Simply Faith

they went and woke him, saying, "Save us, Lord; we are perishing." And he said to them, "Why are you afraid, O you of little faith?" Then he rose and rebuked the winds and the sea, and there was a great calm. And the men marveled, saying, "What sort of man is this, that even winds and sea obey him?"

Mark 4:1-41 ESV

Again, he began to teach beside the sea. And a very large crowd gathered about him, so that he got into a boat and sat in it on the sea, and the whole crowd was beside the sea on the land.

And he was teaching them many things in parables, and in his teaching he said to them, "Listen! A sower went out to sow. And as he sowed, some seed fell along the path, and the birds came and devoured it. Other seed fell on rocky ground, where it did not have much soil, and immediately it sprang up, since it had no depth of soil. ... shaken.

1 Kings 19:12 ESV

And after the earthquake, a fire, but the LORD was not in the fire. And after the fire, the sound of a low whisper.

1 Peter 5:7 ESV

Casting all your anxieties on him, because he cares for you.

Lamentations 3:25-26 ESV

The LORD is good to those who wait for him, to the soul who seeks him. It is good that one should wait quietly for the salvation of the LORD.

John 14:27 ESV

Peace I leave with you; my peace I give to you. Not as the world gives do I give to you. Let not your hearts be troubled, neither let them be afraid.

John 3:16-17 ESV

"For God so loved the world that he gave his only Son, that whoever believes in him should not perish but have eternal life. For God did not send his Son into the world to condemn the world, but in order that the world might be saved through him.

Psalm 1:1-6 ESV

Blessed is the man who walks not in the counsel of the

wicked, nor stands in the way of sinners, nor sits in the seat of scoffers; but his delight is in the law of the LORD, and on his law he meditates day and night. He is like a tree planted by streams of water that yields its fruit in its season, and its leaf does not wither. In all that he does, he prospers. The wicked are not so but are like chaff that the wind drives away. Therefore, the wicked will not stand in the judgment, nor sinners in the congregation of the righteous; ...

Hebrews 11:1-40 ESV

Now faith is the assurance of things hoped for, the conviction of things not seen. For by it the people of old received their commendation. By faith we understand that the universe was created by the word of God, so that what is seen was not made out of things that are visible. By faith Abel offered to God a more acceptable sacrifice than Cain, through which he was commended as righteous, God commending him by accepting his gifts. And through his faith, though he died, he still speaks. By faith Enoch was taken up so that he should not see death, and he was not found, because God had taken him. Now before he was taken, he was commended as having pleased God. ...

Romans 15:4-5 ESV

For whatever was written in former days was written for our instruction, that through endurance and through the encouragement of the Scriptures we might have hope. May the God of endurance and encouragement grant you to live in such harmony with one another, in accord with Christ Jesus,

Mark 11:24 ESV

Therefore, I tell you, whatever you ask in prayer, believe that you have received it, and it will be yours.

Matthew 7:7 ESV

"Ask, and it will be given to you; seek, and you will find; knock, and it will be opened to you.

Psalm 46:2 ESV

Therefore, we will not fear though the earth gives way, though the mountains be moved into the heart of the sea,

Simply Faith

Joshua 1:8 ESV

This Book of the Law shall not depart from your mouth, but you shall meditate on it day and night, so that you may be careful to do according to all that is written in it. For then you will make your way prosperous, and then you will have good success.

Philippians 4:6-7 ESV

Do not be anxious about anything, but in everything, by prayer and supplication with thanksgiving, let your requests be made known to God. And the peace of God, which surpasses all understanding, will guard your hearts and your minds in Christ Jesus.

Psalm 91:1 ESV

He who dwells in the shelter of the Most High will abide in the shadow of the Almighty.

Genesis 17:1-8, 15-16

God's promises to Abraham and Sarah (Abram was ninety-nine years old).

Genesis 22

The Sacrifice of Isaac

Daniel 3:16-18

Three Hebrew Boys—we should trust God and obey Him even if He does not deliver us. They were all in on the idea that I would rather believe that God can and will than to think otherwise. What were their options? For them, apparently none.

Daniel 6 - Daniel is saved from the Lions

Seed + Water + Soil = Harvest, and the potential harvest is based on the seed. Otherwise, there will not be a yield. Something has to happen for growth. This combination creates the germination process. God has given (deposited in) all of us the seed of faith. It is God making an investment in us with interest. God's deposit has endless potential. When we receive faith, time, and interest, we have equal confidence. For this reason, Hebrews 10:35-35 Cast not away therefore your confidence, which has great recompense of reward. The seeds hold the promise that a harvest is to come. Most seeds are relatively easy to grow; however, all need to be maintained. So do not throw away your confidence; it holds a great reward.

I urge you to read these scriptures with the expectation that you too will be inspired to understand God's desire for you when the vision is blurred.

Scriptures can be compared to a blueprint. It has potential, but there must be (application) work for the structure to become a reality. The good or best part is that except the Lord builds the house, we labor in vain. You see, we never have to go it alone. If there are modifications to be reckoned with, God is able to make change orders when needed. However, he expects us to trust him that the task will be completed. You will be overwhelmed by his willingness to help us when we come to him with an outstretched hand to receive his assistance.

"Come as a little child" is the instruction and example given by Jesus in Matthew 18:2-4. Can it get any simpler? I think not.

What makes the journey difficult is that we do not respond to God promptly. When we become familiar with his voice, then we should respond for that reason. I can recall my mother calling us by name. I may have heard my sister's or brother's name, but I really was listening for my name. "Did you not hear me? she asked." Respectfully, I gave her what I thought was an acceptable reply or excuse. By the way, the excuses were seldom okay. The point is that she knew that I should have been within the sound of her voice. Shouldn't we anticipate this from God as well?

Thankfully, we can never be too far that he or we can't be heard. Let's keep that in mind as a lifetime tutorial. Start a conversation with Him, and you will not be ignored, never. "And Jesus answered and said unto him, "What would you that I should do unto you?" Mark 10:51 and Luke 18:41. Let's give the same consideration to God when he speaks to us. Your tracking number is Proverbs 3:5-7.

Simply Faith
About the Author

Reverend Dr. Linwood Best is pastor emeritus of Christian Fellowship Church. He and his wife Brenda are the proud parents of one daughter and two granddaughters.

Academic bedrock: Northwest Florida State College, Shaw Divinity School, North Carolina Central University, Christian Bible College, and Dallas Theological Seminary.

As a dutiful shepherd in the ministry, his passion and love are to assist the elderly, those that are confined, at risk, and the economically disadvantaged. His aim is to apply biblical truths to the needs of common people and make doctrine practical and exciting. He has, for more than thirty years, provided Bible study for senior citizens. This unique group consists of overlapping convictions and culturally diverse populations. Meeting with them for lunch on Tuesdays for the enrichment of their knowledge of God's word has been the highlight of their week, especially his. It is often said that there are not enough hours in a day. Dr. B. believes that when we listen to the voice of God, we will have ample time to fulfill life's mission.

Dr. Best has received many awards and certificates, but the most cherished are the nominations for public service: the Jefferson and John R. Larkins. This award recognizes a state employee whose work ethic goes above and beyond self-determination and promotes and encourages the same in others. This acknowledgment was a result of him taking action to improve communication and relationships between people of different racial or ethnic groups in the community and workplace.

He has hosted a weekly radio broadcast, "Sowing Seeds," written seven books, copywriter of eleven songs, and the author of more than thirty sonnets and poems.

He believes, "Those who are wise will shine like the brightness of the heavens, and those who lead many to righteousness will shine like the stars forever and ever."

Although faith comes by hearing, we might not get it initially. Like those who followed Jesus, it took time, but they got it, and so will we.

Also, from Empower Publishing
by Linwood Best

Best "Quotes"

Best "Saying"

Best "Thoughts on Paper"

Learn to Listen and Listen to Learn

Made in the USA
Middletown, DE
29 June 2025